PHOENIX

SENI

ENGLI

GUID

Wilfred Owen

PHOENIX SENIOR ENGLISH GUIDES

currently available

Coleridge

The Crucible

Bruce Dawe

The Great Gatsby

Hamlet

Gwen Harwood

Macbeth

Othello

Wilfred Owen

Pride and Prejudice

Robert Frost

Kenneth Slessor

Snow Falling on Cedars

Strictly Ballroom

PHOENIX
SENIOR
ENGLISH
GUIDES

Wilfred Owen

FRANCES RUSSELL MATTHEWS

PHOENIX
EDUCATION

PHOENIX
EDUCATION

First published in Australia in 2000

PHOENIX EDUCATION PTY LTD
PO Box 197, Albert Park 3206
Tel: (03) 9699 8377 Fax: (03) 9699 9242
PO Box 3141, Putney 2112
Tel: (02) 9809 3579 Fax: (02) 9808 1430

ISBN 1 876580 05 4

Text design and page make-up by Graphic Divine
Cover design by Sharon Carr
Cover marbling by Galen Berry
Printed in Australia by Shannon Books

Contents

How to use this book

This book provides you with a structure for getting to know the work of Wilfred Owen. In it you will find a summary of the literary tradition in which his poems were written; a summary of some of his most important subject matter, ideas, themes and techniques; a guide to developing your own response to important examples of his work; some hints on the analysis of individual poems; and a guide for effectively preparing for and writing effectively in exams on Wilfred Owen's poetry.

Chapter 3 'The poems in close-up' offers you three levels of response so that you can confidently develop your *own* response and understanding of Owen's work.

- **Your first response**: This is your record of your initial impressions on first reading and thinking about the poem. You may like to write notes as you read: jot down possible themes, and note effective, surprising or challenging imagery. Observe and tag the effectiveness of the poet's use of sound in individual words, phrases and lines. Note the type and use of rhyme. Try to 'feel' the way the rhythm or metre works. Are there places in the poem where the metre hastens or slows down? Draw some basic conclusions about the poem: Is it sad? Happy? Provocative? Challenging? Does it shock? Terrify? Does it ennoble humanity or criticise it? Is it joyful at the nature of life or thoughtful about its challenges and difficulties? Does it use colour? Are there obvious symbols? Do these symbols form a pattern? Is there a connecting motif such as a journey? How important is contrast? Does the poem develop a thesis about its subject matter? Do you agree with or have sympathy for what the poet's point of view?

- **A closer analysis**: This provides you with a structured, focused analysis of each idea in the poem in turn and asks questions that invite you to draw your own conclusions about theme and technique.

- **Your second response**: Take this opportunity to write at length on the poem. Refer to the text of the poem to select quotes which effectively support your argument. Try to write a coherent discussion on one of the suggested topics – or on one of your own. You can do it! This is your first step to taking hold of the poem and successfully meeting the challenge of its ideas.

Remember: use this text to develop your own ideas, and view all that it says critically. And, if you are preparing for an examination, make sure that your first step is to check out the syllabus, so that you do not find yourself studying the wrong poems or insufficient examples of the Wilfred Owen's work.

1

A guide to the analysis of poetry

Poetry is a very specialised form of communication. Its uniqueness is derived from:

- a sensitivity to the effect of individual sounds, individual words and particular word combinations
- an expression of deeply felt emotions and feelings
- an intensity of thought and a consciousness of thought patterns
- a selectivity of subject matter in order to focus on particular themes
- a structural dependency (often) on particular poetic forms

The analysis of any poem requires you to:

- identify the subject matter and the specific focus of its presentation
- explore the themes developed through the subject matter
- respond to the language used by the poet to encode thoughts, feelings, nuances and suggestions
- develop a sensitivity to the effectiveness of sound and sound patterns
- have an awareness of the individual treatment of an individual genre, where one is used as the structural and thematic base of the poem
- apply the principles of good essay writing: understand the question, and write about it with a specific focus in a well-organised structure

Understanding a poem

To successfully read and understand any poem:

- Take notice of the title (if there is one) – this will define the subject matter of the poem or the poem's thematic focus.
- Create a context for your deeper thoughts about the poem by reading it quickly to gain a first impression. Make notes on this first response.
- Read the poem again – carefully, analytically and out loud. Listen to the sounds of the words and phrases. Attune your hearing to the sound of the rhyme and

1

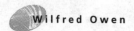

identify the sounds which any pattern of rhyme reinforces. Be sensitive to the tone of the poem, the attitude of the poetic 'voice'. Note its cumulative atmospheric effect. Remember that poetry is essentially sound with meaning.

- Note the impact of the poetic language: identify the particularly effective or discordant or soothing sounds, words and phrases; be aware of sound patterns and of the feelings and sensitivities these evoke in the reader.
- Identify the obvious meaning, then look for implied meaning(s).
- Read the poem again to consolidate your appreciation of its meaning.
- Identify a hierarchy of themes – do not expect the themes to be developed equally.
- Determine how the use of imaginative language, poetic imagery and figures of speech contribute to the portrayal and expansion of the meaning. Identify the visual elements of the poem; clarify the images they evoke in your imagination.
- Be sensitive to the use of setting and atmosphere as symbols of the main themes.

Identifying poetic themes

In order to identify poetic themes, you need to identify the ideas, attitudes, feelings and philosophy presented by the poet through the subject matter of events, characters and philosophy – whether personal, religious or social.

Remember that while some themes are unique to every poem in the personal focus given to their presentation by the poet, many themes are universal to all poetry. These universal themes include:

- the nature of love and its associated happiness, trials and sadness
- the patterns of nature, including the cycle of the seasons
- the nature of idealism and its defeat in the face of reality
- the special world view of young people
- the losses, disenchantment, wisdom and resignation of old age
- the corruption of humankind, including the corrupting influence of ambition, power, fame and greed
- the pain and trauma of grief
- the powerlessness of humankind against time, war and passion
- the futility and brutality of war
- death as the ultimate challenge of the strength of the human spirit
- the value of the individual and the worth of individual lives well lived
- the value of solitude and the pain of loneliness
- the importance of companionship to the human spirit; the value of mateship and of friendship especially at times of trial
- the transience of all things – the inevitability of decay and death for all living things

- the power and nature of arrogance and the strength and value of humility
- the strength of anger and the power of forgiveness
- the special state of motherhood, and the strength of maternal love
- the power of the human imagination
- the often destructive power of religion and the human need for faith
- the eternal struggle between good and evil both within individual men and women and in their external world; the energy of evil; the passivity of goodness
- the value and also the emptiness of patriotism; love of the homeland
- the beauty of the landscape – of its animate and inanimate elements
- the relentless power of the sea
- the anonymity and stresses of urban life
- the bonds of our common humanity
- the indifference of politics to the real needs of man and woman kind
- the struggle of all living creatures to communicate with others

Know your technical terms

Understand the basic techniques of each poem which you are studying. This will give you a basis for your analysis and provide a guide to the nature of the ideas and of the emotions to be examined in it.

If you understand the basic techniques of the poem, you can discuss its style and, more importantly, the integration and interaction of style and meaning.

Develop your own personal working analytical vocabulary through the effective use of technical terms. Some important technical terms for you to identify and understand are listed below.

allegory: literally 'other meaning'. In allegory, characters, incidents and setting operate on many levels. What is depicted as the life of an individual may represent a universal statement about the life of Everyman. The story of a wanderer may represent the journeys made by all people living out their individual lives. In 'The Show', a dead man's view of his own corpse becomes a statement for the foulness of the entire battlefield. In 'Miners', the Halmerend mining disaster becomes a statement for society's endorsement of the sacrifice of the lives of some individuals in war and peace time to ensure the luxury and comfort of others.

alliteration: literally 'more letters'. Alliteration is the repetition of sounds (mostly consonants), usually at the beginning of words or of stressed syllables. It creates atmosphere, and emphasises the poet's ideas and feelings by the sounds it interweaves in the poetic line. It is thus both a structural and semantic element.

Alliteration of 's' is a structural and atmospheric element of 'Futility', defining the sense of helplessness of the speaker and all men in the face of the carnage of the battlefield. In 'Mental Cases' the alliteration of 's' defines the slobbering state of the mental cases and the disgust of their observer. In 'The Sentry' the alliteration of 'b' defines the despair of the blinded sentry.

archetype: a character, image or storyline which is found repeatedly in myth and throughout literary tradition. The blinded sentry of 'The Sentry' is the archetypal scapegoat of the politicians whose ambitions drive the war. The journey from life into the world of death is the archetypal situation of 'The Show' and 'Strange Meeting'. The battle of 'Spring Offensive' is the archetypal battle which defines humanity's callousness to itself and to nature.

assonance: literally 'the answer to'. It is the correspondence (or near correspondence) in two words of the stressed vowel, and sometimes also of the following vowels. This method of creating patterns in sound is a common feature of English verse, and often adds dramatic intensity to a poem, giving it a coherence of sound that is married to the coherence of ideas.

Owen delights in the patterns of sound that assonance creates, and exploits its effect fully, using it particularly effectively in his evocation of the sounds of the battlefield. In 'From My Diary, July 1914', each of the long lines contains elaborate assonance or alliteration or both.

ballad: the traditional ballad has given modern poetry a sense of drama, a vivid exploitation of dialogue, a simple stanza form of four lines, a sense of lilting rhythm, and an appreciation of rhyme in reinforcing the metrical and semantic patterns. A ballad opens abruptly as the setting and the action are swiftly and economically drawn. It repeats key ideas and key events, often in a refrain.

In the vividness of his images and in his appreciation of rhyme and rhythm and in his use of patterns and repetitions, Owen has drawn on the ballad tradition.

blank verse: unrhymed verse, often written in iambic pentameters (five metrical feet, of ten syllables). It mimics natural speech, although it is a little more sophisticated.

conceit: a figure of speech which establishes a startling comparison between two apparently quite dissimilar ideas or images. Powerful conceits to be found in Owen's work are that of the individual corpse as a metaphor for the entire battlefield in 'The Show' and artillery fire as snow in 'Futility'. In 'Apologia pro Poemate Meo', stanzas five and six describe the bonding of soldiers in images of ribbon and kisses which are taken from love poetry.

dramatic monologue: the spoken expression of the poet as the main character. The speaker addresses one or more people who are not heard in the poem but whose emotions and reactions are responded to or foreshadowed by the speaker. The speaker's character is revealed by the content and structure of what he or she says. 'A Terre' is a powerful exploitation of this poetic form.

elegy: a formal lament for the death of an individual, or for human mortality or for the transience of all things that are meaningful for humankind. 'Anthem for Doomed Youth' is a deservedly famous elegy which captures the sadness of those left at home and the special poignancy of death on the battlefield.

enjambment: the flow-on of one poetic line into the next without a break and the consequent flow-on of ideas and feeling.

epic: a long narrative on a serious subject, told with a sense of ceremony in formal speech which is elevated in style. The setting is a comprehensive one, spanning hell, earth and heaven. The action is heroic and often involves super-human feats. The main character faces many difficulties.

epigram: a poem of two or three lines which makes a succinct, often witty comment on a subject.

figurative language: the imaginative use of language so that it has a more than literal meaning. Personification, simile and metaphor are examples.

free verse: poetic utterance which does not conform to technical patterns of metre, rhyme or genre.

heroic couplets: rhyming pairs of lines, each with five units each consisting of an unstressed syllable followed by a stressed syllable. Heroic couplets were used by Shakespeare to round off his sonnets.

imagery: the imaginative pictures created by the words of a poem. Imagery appeals to all five senses: sight, sound, touch, taste and hearing. Imagery is also the term used to describe the effect of figurative language. The imagery of Owen's poems is particularly notable for the range of sensory experience it evokes in its definition of the special hell of the Western Front, and in particular of trench and gas warfare. The sea imagery of 'The Sentry' is particularly memorable.

metaphor: a comparison of one thing, quality or action to another by directly stating that it *is* the other. It is a compact form of imagery, an intensified thought, which expands in the imagination. It has a philosophical and intellectual confidence and often introduces a sense of drama.

metre: the regular rhythm given to a poem by the stresses of its words in isolation and in combination. Metre is the backbone or scaffolding of a poem's meaning.

ode: a long lyric poem, serious in subject, formal in style and complicated in verse pattern. Odes are poems of praise or of contemplation. 'Insensibility' exploits this form to define the categories of all who are deadened by the experience of war.

onomatopoeia: a word or combination of words whose sound recreates the sound it denotes. Owen exploits this technique fully in bringing into his verse the actual sound of both sniper fire, heavy artillery and gas canisters.

pastoral: traditionally, a Greek poem written about the lives of shepherds and shepherdesses. Today, the term is applied to any poem which celebrates the

simple joys of simple lives led by ordinary working people. There is a strong pastoral element in 'Futility'.

persona: literally 'a mask'. The persona is the narrative voice, the point of view of a poem which is clearly not that of the poet. These first-person narrators are deliberate constructions by the poet to achieve a particular purpose in an individual poem. The personae of Owen's poems are particularly confronting as many speak out of immediate battlefield experience or from close association with the wounded or as the wounded.

personification: assigning the qualities and feelings of a living being to an inanimate object. It thereby provides an imaginative expansion of the poem and is often a key to a poet's exploration of the meaning of universal themes.

poetic diction: the combination of the words, phrases, and figurative language of a poem. Poets often give individual characters their own distinctive diction. A particular poet's work is often characterised by favourite words or turns of phrase. In Owen's poetry, the simplicity of the persona's utterance in 'Futility' and the grim objectivity of the persona's voice in 'The Show' each contribute much to the dramatic effectiveness of these poems.

pun: a play on words to create a joke with meaning.

rhyme: the agreement of two metrically accented syllables in their vowel sounds and final consonants. Any unaccented syllables that follow the accented syllables must be identical.

rhyme scheme: the pattern created by rhyme in the last words of each line. The pattern is described by giving a letter of the alphabet (a,b,c. ... z) to each end-rhyme.

satire: a satirical poem uses comedy as a weapon to promote laughter at the object or person or event so derided. By means of such laughter, readers are brought to recognise their own potential to commit the same error or to demonstrate the same egotistical action.

simile: a comparison between two different things using 'like' or 'as'.

sonnet: a one-stanza lyric poem of fourteen lines linked by a complex rhyme scheme. Love was the traditional subject. However, sonnets are now used to deal (either seriously or comically) with almost any subject in an elevated, formal way. Sonnets are characterised by intensity of thought and, often, a sense of drama. 'Anthem of Doomed Youth' exploits the power of this poetic form.

Understanding poetic metre

A poetic line is a row of syllables. Each syllable has a metrical value – a degree of emphasis – which, when scanned, will give you the metrical pattern of the line. The simplest pattern is that between stressed and unstressed syllables. Together these provide the metrical scheme of the poem.

Stress is emphasis, the degree of loudness given to the articulation of any sound. Additional contributory factors are pitch; the duration or length of the sound; and the weightiness given to the sounds by the individual consonants. The relative amount of stress given to each syllable reflects the modification of its normal pronunciation by logical demands of the ideas being presented and their emotional emphases.

The simplest means of marking stress patterns is the use of a slanting stroke to mark the major stresses in a line and a cross to mark the weak stresses. The patterns created by these strong and weak stresses fall into groups called metrical feet which are made up of a combination of two or three syllables, only one of which is stressed.

The kinds of metrical feet thus created have names adopted from classical sources. The most important are shown below:

Name	Syllable pattern	Written as:	Example
iamb	unstressed–stressed	X/	*intense*
trochee	stressed–unstressed	/X	*feather*
anapaest	unstressed–unstressed–stressed	XX/	*refugee*
amphibrach	unstressed–stressed–unstressed	X/X	*resemble*
dactyl	stressed–unstressed–unstressed	/XX	*magical*

These metrical patterns allow us to formally characterise the poet's use of the rhythms of everyday speech. The most common metrical pattern is the iambic pattern. The next most common is the other two-syllable pattern, the trochee. Any variation from the usual iambic metre will provide metrical emphasis to the words (and therefore the ideas) which are differently and unexpectedly accented. Other elements of variety are added to the poetic line by:

- a pause in the middle of the line (marked by a dash or a full stop or colon) known as *caesura*
- the patterns of sound created by the use of rhyme, usually a combination of assonance and alliteration
- the use of enjambment
- the interweaving of monosyllabic and trisyllabic words within the standard iambic line
- the use of couplets (two adjacent rhymed lines) which provide distinct units of sense

The poet in close-up

Wilfred Owen – the man

- Born 18 March 1893, at Oswestry, in England, the eldest of four children, into a poor middle-class family, to be adored by his mother and distanced from his father who worked for the railways.
- Instructed in evangelical Anglicanism with its emphasis on the paramount importance of faith, the redeeming sacrifice of the crucified Christ and the importance of prayer and Bible reading.
- Spent the greater part of his childhood years in the industrial city of Birkenhead.
- In 1907, moved to rural Shrewsbury near the Roman ruins of Uriconium.
- A good scholar, who preferred his books to physical boyhood pursuits.
- First employed as a junior teacher at an elementary school.
- In 1911 passed the entrance examination for London University, but achieved insufficient marks to be awarded a scholarship.
- Became lay assistant to the Vicar of Dunsden, Oxfordshire.
- Began to write sonnets and exchanged them with his friends, Owen and Leslie Gunston, and his cousin, Olwen Joergens; these early works include 'Happiness', 'Music', 'The End' and 'My Shy Hand'.
- Developed a close friendships with the boys of the Dunsden parish.
- In 1912, read a life of Shelley and found in it some of the same questioning of Anglican orthodoxy which he himself was increasingly feeling.
- Began to question the rigorous condemnation of humankind in the orthodoxy of the Fall and in the Anglican belief that all are damned unless converted to the active practice of religious faith; such a crisis of conscience caused him to leave the Vicarage in February 1913, and return to Shrewsbury, having abandoned the Church forever.
- Was beset by nightmares.
- His brother Harold joined the navy.

- Moved to France in late 1913, where he taught English at Bordeaux.
- In July 1914, became private tutor to the children of the Légers family, in the French Pyrenees.
- Met and was befriended by the poet Laurent Tailhade.
- Left the Légers in August, 1914, to obtain a similar post where he remained until August 1915.
- On 21 October 1915 enlisted in the Artists' Rifles with whom he trained in England until December 1916, when he took a commission in the Manchester Regiment.
- Befriended poet Harold Monro.
- December 1916, embarked for France.
- Reflected his first posting to no-man's-land near Beaumont Hamel in 'The Sentry' and 'Exposure'.
- March 1917, transferred to a Casualty Clearing Station for treatment for concussion, the result of a fall, rather than a war injury.
- April 1917, had a twelve day stint in action in the attack on Fayet, where he was injured by a shell; was returned to the Casualty Clearing Station suffering from shell shock; he was thereafter plagued by the horrors of trench warfare.
- Invalided back home to Craiglockhart War Hospital, Edinburgh, where he was to spend the next four months; wrote prolifically but was plagued by nightmares through which he relived his battlefield experiences.
- July, 1917, became editor of the Craiglockhart War Hospital magazine.
- August 1917, the poet Siegfried Sassoon became a fellow patient.
- October, 1917, Owen was discharged from hospital, counting himself, at last, a poet.
- Posted to the management of barracks at Scarborough.
- August, 1918, returned to the Front.
- After a fortnight or so behind the lines, Owen returned to battle by his own choice, where his gallantry and devotion to duty earned him the Military Cross
- Was killed on 4 November 1918; one week later, the war was over.

Wilfred Owen — his times

Wilfred Owen grew up in a world that glorified the British Empire and held fast to patriotic and romantic ideals arising out of a nostalgia for its past grandeur and great military victories. His England saw herself as the defender of the Christian faith and of European democracy, ideals in the promotion of which it was prepared to sacrifice a whole generation of its young men — and in particular its young gentleman soldiers who were lauded for their bravery, stoicism, sense of honour and preparedness to sacrifice themselves in the protection of its way of life.

At the heart of power in 1914 Europe were the political leaders of the European States, deeply divided and dominated by alliances.

In 1914 Germany, Austria and Hungary were still members of the Triple Alliance formed in 1882, each state pledged to defend the other. On the other side, France and Russia were aligned in a pact of mutual defence. France and Britain were joined in the Entente Cordial. In their internal domestic politics, none of these countries had yet achieved universal suffrage or a parliamentary system as we now know it. Unlike Australia and New Zealand, no European state had yet given women the vote.

Political power was exercised in Britain by an elite drawn from the upper-middle class and aristocracy. Like its European counterparts, however, it had domestic problems, in Britain's case, the Irish problem and a growing and increasingly politically minded mass labour movement demanding economic, social and political rights for ordinary working people. Socialist movements were also active, demanding a transformation of capitalism into a more equitable and just social order. Issues of nationality and class deeply divided European society before and after the war.

The second power base in World War I was composed of the men who directed military and naval affairs. To a great extent the War was 'the General's War'.

The social composition of the general staffs of the major European armies of the time were very similar. Most were members of the untitled or titled gentry, who had attended the military academies of their countries. Some had seen service in colonial wars; the arts of manoeuvre in which they had been schooled had a traditional basis in cavalry warfare.

As the armies had expanded in the first decade of the twentieth century, the officer corps had been democratised by the admission to their ranks of middle-class men, needed to process the increasing numbers of recruits.

In Britain as elsewhere in Europe, army and nation had grown closer together. Political policies saw military action as the solution to political problems; offensive strategies were preferred against defensive strategies. In all, the infantry was seen as the key element in what all believed would be a short action. 'The Great Adventure' which World War 1 was first known highlighted the deficiencies in both the politics and the military tactics which supported them.

Behind the armies and the politicians and officers was the Home Front. This Front supplied the masses of soldiers and sailors who became the cannon fodder serving political principle.

When the war broke out in August 1914, with the German invasion of France, it was a war of illusions, which most believed would be short and relatively uncostly in effort and manpower. In Britain, the higher a man was up on the social scale, the more likely it was that he would enlist early and serve throughout the conflict. Roughly six million British men would eventually serve in the conflict. The majority of them were working class. As the bloodshed worsened, the high casualty rate amongst officers meant that begrudgingly men from the lower middle class and working class were accepted into the officer corps. For all of them, the smell, sound and chaos of war was not what they had expected.

In France and Flanders, the front was not one line but many. The British system of trench warfare was fairly regular. Facing the enemy lines was the fire trench, built to a zig-zag pattern to deaden explosions and to prevent deadly fire from the flank from traversing the line. The trench was deep enough to avoid shrapnel danger but was ineffective in offering protection from sniper fire. Its floor was covered by wooden duckboards – and not long after the commencement of hostilities with the dead. There was no time for burial.

At times the enemy line was no more than 45 metres away. Frequently 'no-man's-land' between them was penetrated by listening posts. The second line of trenches lay behind the first. This was the support line, connected to by a communication trench to those behind.

The German trench system was more complex. Deep bunkers offered protection from the bombardment which preceded enemy attacks. It was from these that the German soldiers emerged with their machine guns to annihilate the advancing lines of troops.

In the first five months of the war, appalling casualties decimated both sides. The French army lost approximately 400,000 men killed between August and December 1914. German losses on the Western Front were lower, but it also lost approximately 140,000 men on the Eastern Front. Russian losses were greater still.

By 1915, the battle lines had hardened, early victory had eluded the Germans, and the Western Front – a series of linked fortifications across southern Belgium and northern France from the English Channel to the Swiss border – had been produced. It was here, rather than on the vast Eastern Front in Poland and the Balkans, where the war was to either to be won or lost.

On 22 April 1915, poison gas was used for the first time in the war. German troops opened 6000 canisters of chlorine along an 8-kilometre front near Ypres. The French and Algerian troops who were not suffocated by it, fled. Two days later, the Canadians were gassed. In May, it was the British turn, but a sudden change in wind caused casualties on both sides. By 1918, roughly one in four shells fired on the Western Front was a gas shell. Chlorine had been joined by the more lethal phosgene and mustard gas, the latter a forerunner of napalm. Box respirators became standard field equipment. Those who fell victim to it suffered great serrating blisters with blind eyes all sticky and stuck together, and throats that choked as lungs collapsed. The lucky ones would regain their sight in a few

hours. Most, however, were blinded for life, with lungs so badly damaged that recovery was extremely painful. Medical science of the time had no cure for its effects.

The first military gamble in the war was made by Germany in 1914 when it invaded France. The second began in February 1916 when it tried to bleed the French army white by an assault on the salient of Verdun in eastern France. On the first day of the assault, more than a million shells fell on French positions, clustered around a series of forts on both sides of the River Meuse. Almost the entire French infantry fought to hold Verdun, a city of no real strategic importance but whose loss would have been, for the French generals, a political catastrophe. This battle turned into a ten-month bloodbath for both sides.

While the fighting around Verdun raged, the British opened a major offensive further west in France, near the River Somme. The assault was launched on 1 July 1916, and was renewed periodically throughout the following six months with no success in its primary objective which was to break through German lines in order to fight a war of movement rather than of stalemate. Wave upon wave of infantrymen left their trenches only to be slaughtered by German machine gunners. This pattern continued for six months. By the end of the first day, the British army had suffered 60,000 casualties, of whom one-third had been killed. This was the worst day of carnage suffered by the British in its military history. British and French casualties together exceeded 620,000. German casualties reached 450,000.

In late July 1916, the British tried again in southern Belgium, near the city of Ypres. This series of offensive operations dragged on until November. It is called the Third Battle of Ypres, or simply Passchendale. It too was a complete failure as the German defensive positions held out. The cost to both sides of the entire battle was approximately two million casualties. The British lost some 40,000 men on the first day. Total casualties passed 500,000. The British had fought and lost two battles: against the Germans and against the elements. Heavy rain turned the battlefield into glutinous mud which impeded any advance.

The British were successful, however, in maintaining a blockade of German ports. In the Battle of Jutland, Britain kept control of the North Sea. This, with poor harvests, brought the German population to the point of starvation, and forced it to undertake the third gamble of the War its submarine offensive.

In April 1917, the United States declared war on the Central Powers in response to the German U-boat campaign. This and the Russian Revolution in March 1917 changed the character of the war. The latter led, with the seizure of power by Lenin and the revolutionary Bolshevik socialists, to the Russians signing the Treaty of Brest-Litovsk on 3 March 1918, under which the Russians handed over to Germany a vast territory including Poland, the Ukraine, the

Baltic states and Finland, thus creating a huge German Eastern Empire.

Germany could now concentrate its efforts on the Western Front. It launched a new offensive on 21 March 1918 in France and Belgium in an all-out effort to win the war before America's influence could be felt. It had developed an attack-in-depth system, avoiding the Allied approach of breaking or defending a rigid line. The German strategy called for sudden gas and artillery barrages to disrupt and demoralise the enemy, followed by the use of storm troop infiltration attacks. German columns again marched towards Paris.

The German army came within 80 kilometres of Paris but could not capitalise on its gains. It ran out of manpower and resources just as the Americans were making their influence felt. By the summer of 1918, the tide had turned. The German army began its retreat. By the summer of 1918, Germany's allies had collapsed. The German high command was faced with mass surrenders and a collapse of morale which was repeated too on the German home front. The Kaiser abdicated and the armistice took effect on 11 November 1918.

The aftermath of the war was a time of reckoning and of mourning for millions of people around the world. Its victims became the Lost Generation.

Wilfred Owen – his work

While the final judgment of the nature and achievement of Wilfred Owen's work is a matter for your own discernment, consider, as you read and study his work, the following favourite subjects, themes and techniques of the poet:

- the empty idealism of those who first enlisted for the war and those who lauded their doing so
- the collapse of the romantic myth of chivalry and of an honourable war in the face of the reality of the Western Front
- the hideous landscapes, and the ugliness, stench, deafening sound and ever-present danger of the battlefield
- the carnage of war which mocks blind patriotism by a human catastrophe of gigantic proportions
- the questioning of Christ's presence on the battlefield
- the ultimate test of individual strength, courage and compassion on the battle-field
- the annihilation of civilisation
- the hollowness of political propaganda
- the distortion of death and of the dead on the battlefield
- the strength of man's desire to live
- no-man's-land as the abode of madness

- the enduring psychological legacy of war
- the conscious selection of specific words for their special individual effect, creating by their use, particular points of semantic and technical significance in the poems
- a deliberateness in the use of rhyme, half-rhyme and pararhyme making sound part of the actual meaning of each poem rather than a mere vehicle conveying ideas
- use of colour as a semantic and often symbolic focal point in the progress of the poem's ideas
- an appreciation of the semantic strength and dramatic effect achievable in the simplicity of carefully chosen monosyllables
- the exploitation of traditional Romantic images of nature, the sun, flowers, music, spring and the weather to express the carnage of the battlefield
- the exploitation of rhetoric and of dialogue to define the battlefield experience

3

The poems in close-up

'Maundy Thursday'

This sonnet provides an examination from the perspective of the altar rail of the mixed motivations and reluctant or simple faith of those members of the congregation who present themselves for Communion, and an insight into the dying faith of Owen himself.

BEFORE YOU READ

- Investigate the symbolism of the crucifix in Catholic orthodox belief.
- Examine your own practice of religion. Is it more a matter of observance and of public performance than sincere belief?
- Attend a Catholic communion service.
- Read up on the sonnet form.
- Research the meaning of Maundy Thursday.

YOUR FIRST RESPONSE

A CLOSER ANALYSIS

The first two lines establish the physical and spiritual reality of the poem: we are in the midst of the communion service. What is the effect of the speaker's use of the adjective 'brown'? What insight does it provide into the everyday lives of the congregation? A suggestion of lives lived outdoors? Hard toil? Lives lived in close association with the earth?

Is there a significance in the fact that it is the server boy's hands which are given prominence in the first line over the 'silver cross' of the next line? What is suggested by the use of 'silver'? The gleam of a religious ornament? A coldness? A demanding physical reality?

The men come first – a statement perhaps of the social hierarchy which operates in their community. Their physical heaviness and ungainliness are captured in the heavy awkward combinations of sounds and slow rhythm of 'lugubrious'. Is their awkwardness merely physical? Or is there some suggestion also of difficulties of the heart and of the spirit? Are these the kinds of difficulties denoted in the reluctant and 'half-prejudiced' way by which their act of kneeling is described?

The men kissed the crucifix. Is it nevertheless their enthusiasm for their religion captured in the repetition of 'kissed' and 'kissing' – or is it the depth of their pretence? What insight into the sincerity or otherwise of the speaker's own feelings about his faith are denoted by his choice of the word 'emblem'? Does the use of brackets recast this central act of faith into an aside? What contribution to this sidelining of the people's faith is made by the speaker's use of the indefinite article ('a') before creed. Has he lost all certainty of faith?

The women follow their men. What images are suggested by the description of their 'mourning'? Bescarved women with heads bowed? Drab dress? Sorrowfulness of attitude? Quiet solemnity? The need to seek comfort for personal griefs?

The image of the women's 'meek mouths' is given a dramatic reality by the alliteration of 'm'. What else is suggested of the poet's attitude to the active piety of the female worshippers? A deeply felt disdain? An envy felt at the observance of the strength of others' faith when his is weakening? Is it the strength of the women's faith which is presented in the next line? Unlike their husbands (and the speaker) they kiss more than an emblem – rather they embrace with apt meekness, the 'Body of the Christ indeed'. Is the 'indeed' of this line ambiguous? Does it not at one and the same time emphasise the belief of the worshippers and the scepticism of the speaker?

Next to approach the crucifix are the children. It is only they who rejoice in the religious ritual – and it is only their lips which are 'eager'. The contrast between the happiness they derive from their faith and that of their parents refreshes the spirit – until the reason for their joy is explained in line 9. Christ is but a bright silver doll for them. They are yet to find faith at all.

Last to kneel before the acolyte is the speaker. The position he adopts vis a vis the crucifix has none of the humility, and his attitude none of the reverence, meekness or joy of his fellow congregation members. He positions himself above the crucifix. The Christ of his vision is 'thin, cold, and very dead'.

NOTE
- the certainty of lost faith captured in the use of 'very' to the devastation denoted in 'dead'
- the compounding of the sense of loss by the cumulative effect of the conjunction of simple, harsh adjectives
- the significant emphasis on the depth of the speaker's hypocrisy by the alliterative 'yet' and 'yea'
- the touch of sordidness in the too long embrace by the speaker's lips of the warm hands of the server-lad. Does the embrace suggest more than the speaker's consciousness of the contrast between his dying faith and the living boy? Has one passion replaced the other? Is the intimated homosexuality of the image merely there to capture the depth of the speaker's sense of alienation from his religion? Or does it explain the reasons for his alienation?

The techniques

Consider the contribution made to the development of the poem's ideas and subject matter by:
- the symbolic use of colour
- the metrical effect, the sounds and the semantic connotation of 'lugubrious'
- the use of qualifying words such as 'half' in line 4, 'immensely' in line 9, 'very' in line 12
- specific word choice of 'emblem', 'acolyte', and the concluding 'thing'.
- the use of sonnet form
- the use of the conjunction 'and' in line 12
- the use of rhyme
- the use of contrast: between the different levels of faith of the different members of the congregation; between age and youth; between the warmth of the hand and the coldness of the crucifix in line 14

The themes

Consider the following thematic possibilities:
- the different nature of the faith of men, women and children
- the bitterness of the sceptic
- the pain of loss of faith
- the gulf between the physicality of the emblem of the crucifix and its spiritual reality
- the suffering of the crucified Christ
- the hypocrisy which can be present in religious practice
- the strength of affection which can exist between man and boy
- the rebellious spirit who seeks after that which is forbidden by social and religious mores

The universal elements

The poem explores the difficult challenge of reaching and maintaining genuine faith. It explores, too, the isolation felt by the unbeliever in the midst of believers, and his jealous resentment of those who still appear to have at least some vestige of what he has lost.

YOUR SECOND RESPONSE

1. 'In 'Maundy Thursday' Owen lacks the control of a polished poet, allowing his own bitterness to colour too deeply the images he seeks to portray.' Closely analyse the poetic diction, and the imagery of this poem in order to illustrate your view on the accuracy or otherwise of this statement.
2. Does 'Maundy Thursday' have anything of importance to say beyond its analysis of the behaviour of one particular Anglican congregation?
3. 'Maundy Thursday' has been judged a light-hearted commentary on Catholic religious service. Do you agree with this view?

'Shadwell Stair'

'Shadwell Stair' demonstrates Owen's early mastery of the macabre, and his delight in strong, confronting protagonists.

BEFORE YOU READ

- Locate Shadwell Stair in the Pool of London on a map of London.
- Research the Gothic tradition.
- Read Oscar Wilde's 'Impression du Matin', which some critics have suggested Owen imitates in this poem.

YOUR FIRST RESPONSE

A CLOSER ANALYSIS

The poem derives immediate dramatic power from the fact that it is the voice of the ghost itself which is its persona – a fact that the full end-stopping of line 1 invites the reader to contemplate. What additional dramatic effect is gained from the cold matter-of-fact tone with which the speaker narrates the details of the course of his ghostly haunting in lines 2 to 4? What is the particular effect of the rhymes? Of the redefinition of the 'ghost' of line 1 as the 'shadow' in line 4? How more dire is the 'slaughter-house' because of its 'cavernous' nature?

The 'Yet' of line 5 is confronting, the ideas it introduces denying the reader the opportunity created by the ghost's description in the first stanza, of dismissing the ghost as merely an ineffectual, and therefore unthreatening shadow. The speaker asserts his physical reality in this second stanza, his substance defined by an extended simile. The adjectives of line 5 invite the reader's imaginative touch; the extended comparison of the speaker's eyes with the 'moons and lamps in the full Thames' demand visual realisation. What is the effect of the repeated emphasis on the roundness of the ghost's eyes? And of the adjective 'tumultuous', its denotation of movement caught up again in the 'wavering' of line 8? A sense of greater dreadfulness in the fact that the ghost's eyes live rather than merely being passive elements of its visage? Is it their sparkle which the poet wishes to capture foremost? Their evil glittering? Their capacity to pierce the gloom even as the flash of a gem can? What is the atmosphere established by this image? A surreal world of wavering mists where the real and the unreal co-mingle?

The 'shuddering' of the street-arc is given prominence by the placement of the verb at the beginning of line 9. Is there an ambivalence in its movement? Perhaps as a characteristic of the gas that feeds it? Perhaps in response to the ghost's presence? Is not purple also the colour of a corpse?

The atmosphere of eeriness is given a dramatic edge by the speaker's advice that he watches 'always'. The pool's environs provide the right milieu for such attentiveness, the shipping 'clanks' provide the requisite conventional sounds of ghostly chains. This ghost is more than a fleshy presence, however. It has real power: 'And after me a strange tide turns.' Like the street-arcs, the Thames' tides also respond to its being.

Lines 13 and 14 catalogue the duration of the speaker's perambulation, its conclusion marked by the waning of the stars and its progress matched by the parallel creeping of the dawn up the Shadwell Stair. Lines 15 and 16 bring the speaker's dissertation to a surprisingly gentle end. He is driven back to his grave and to the quiet companionship of another ghost by the 'crowing syrens blare'.

The techniques

Consider the contribution made to the development of the poem's ideas and subject matter by:

- the use of full end-stopping to add dramatic weight to the semantic content of the lines
- the contribution made to the physical evocation of the ghost by the physical reality and accuracy of the poem's geography

- the twists and surprises created by the contrast between the image of the speaker ghost evoked in stanzas one and two, and between the powerfulness of its presence explored in stanza three and the quietness with which it returns to its rest
- the use of colour
- the sensory range of the imagery
- the personality given to the ghost by the description of its face

The themes

Consider the following thematic possibilities:

- the other world of the Thames waterside at night
- the reality of the spiritual world
- isolation, alienation and loneliness
- the brashness of commerce
- the beauty of the night
- the possibility of communication with the spirit world – and the consequent suspension of our fear

The universal elements

The poem is grounded in a particular place but explores, nevertheless, the possibility that ghosts share our physical world, attesting to some greater reality than that represented by daytime commerce.

YOUR SECOND RESPONSE

1. 'An effective combination of visual and auditory elements giving life to a ghost.' Is this the achievement of Owen here? Write a critical analysis of the poem, highlighting its weaknesses (if you believe there are some) as well as its strengths.
2. What insight into Owen's developing poetic expertise is provided by 'Shadwell Stair'? Does this poem also suggest a certain fondness of the poet for particular subject matter?
3. Is 'Shadwell Stair' just a lighthearted transplantation of the Gothic to the banks of the Thames?

'From My Diary, July 1914'

This poem celebrates the joys of peace, particularly as the poet experienced them during the first days of his time in the Pyrenees before the outbreak of World War I.

BEFORE YOU READ

- Read about the geography of the Pyrenees.
- Revise the nature and effect of the following techniques: half-rhyme, pararhyme, alliteration and assonance.

YOUR FIRST RESPONSE

A CLOSER ANALYSIS

The poem is a catalogue of sensory experience which demonstrates the poet's delight in and close observation of a specific place.

NOTE

- the plenitude, movement, and visual, auditory and tactile nature of the leaves
- the sense of freshness and freedom of the spirit of the wakening lives
- the liveliness of the birdsong of the dawn and its particular illustration of the joyfulness of the wakefulness in this particular environment
- the rustic pastoral simplicity of the haycutters echoed in their song
- the activity of the bees echoing the activity of man in the previous lines
- the youthful exuberance of the boys as they use their energy in play in contrast to the dark secretiveness of the ebony pond
- the contrasting flashes of light created by the swimmers' movement across the darkness of the pond; the deliberateness of 'carving'; the reality of 'cold'
- the ennobling of the flesh of the swimmers by the golden touch of the sun; the contrast between the gold of the sun and the black of the pool
- the liveliness of the brooks which encircle the mead
- the sharing of mutual attraction between the maid and the speaker
- the throbbing of human hearts reflected in the throbbing of the heat of the landscape
- the warmth of the upland caught in the warmth of the maid's cheek
- the maid's braided hair possibly caught in the braiding of the sun flashes; the sense of companionship, of the intermingling of life
- the quiet stillness that also exists in this energised landscape; the presence of pathos
- the coming of evening; the dying day and the dying flowers; nature's cycle comes full circle
- the beauty of the stars parallelled on earth by the beauty of nocturnal flowers

The techniques

Consider the contribution made to the development of the poem's ideas and subject matter by:

- the interconnecting of the ideas
- the use of alliteration, assonance, rhyme and pararhyme
- the predominance of the progressive aspect ('ing' verbs') capturing the likeliness and energy of both animate and inanimate elements of the landscape
- the powerful effect of contrast
- the combination of visual, auditory, tactile, olfactory elements in the imagery

The themes

Consider the following thematic possibilities:

- the beauty and animation of the Pyrenees landscape
- the simple joys of a pastoral existence
- the magic of freedom
- the positiveness by which the hopeful heart deals with life
- the special freedoms of childhood
- the joy that can be found in work
- the universality of human attraction
- the attractiveness of humanity living in touch with nature
- the plenitude of creation, the magic and variety of life

The universal elements

While evoking the special beauty of life in the Pyrenees, Owen captures the special joys of lives simply and joyfully lived.

YOUR SECOND RESPONSE

1. There is no certain evidence that this poem was actually written by Owen just after his arrival in the Pyrenees and just before the outbreak of war. As a celebration of the beauty of a place and of the joys of freedom, does it really matter?
2. 'The images of 'From My Dairy, July 1914' have the extra poignancy of innocent joy lost.' Do you agree? How powerful is the imagery of the poem?

'Sonnet, on seeing a piece of our heavy artillery'

This sonnet plunges the reader into the reality of the battlefield, where men's lives are subject to forces which are much greater than themselves.

BEFORE YOU READ

- Research the kinds of heavy artillery used by both sides in World War I.
- Revise the principles of the sonnet form.

A CLOSER ANALYSIS

The first two lines of the poem's opening establish the confronting principles of the poem's meaning: the confrontation between human aggression and Heaven's edict for peace. The adverb of the first phrase of line 1 establishes the gun's heaviness (this characteristic is again the foundation of the alliteration and the metre of the first two words of line 3); the reference to its blackness, its evil purpose. The gun is majestic and demanding in its affront to Heaven – its intent defined in the poet's word choice: it is about to 'curse.' Yet the gun is raised with noble purpose – 'against them' (the German enemy).

What is achieved by the poet's use of the abstract to define the enemy as 'Arrogance'? Is his intent merely to sustain the rhetorical mode of the development of the his ideas? Or does the word act as a damning label of the motivation of German aggression? The enemy must be beaten down by the gun, whose voice epitomises the direction of the Allies' resources against him. Is its mission ennobled by the reference to 'gold'?

The sestet is less admiring in tone, as the poet contemplates the consequences of the use of the gun's firepower. Its spell once cast, its blasting charm of line 11 having had its effect, the gun must be purged from the soul of those whose prosperity it has safeguarded. Its evil wickedness must be cursed by God and man alike.

The techniques

Consider the contribution made to the development of the poem's ideas and subject matter by:

- the contrasting ideas of the octave and the sestet
- the poet's use of rhetorical questions
- the underlying imagery of spells and black magic

The themes

Consider the following thematic possibilities:

- the arrogance of German aggression
- the special black magic which must be befriended by those who seek to preserve their way of life against German aggression

- the necessity of meeting violence with violence
- the tainting of the souls of all human beings who are willing or unwilling participants in war
- the cost and curses of warfare
- the sacrifice of the innocent in war
- the sacrifice of Christian principle in war

The universal elements

The monstrous artillery of World War I is both ennobled and damned in this poem as a symbol of the nature and consequence of all warfare, the chief cause of which is human arrogance.

YOUR SECOND RESPONSE

1. Assess the effectiveness and the appropriateness of Owen's clear division of the octave and the sestet of this sonnet.
2. This poem is a portrait of a debate between an inanimate earthbound piece of machinery and God in His Heaven. Is it a less or more effective poem for its sidelining of humanity? Illustrate your view by close attention to the techniques as well as the ideas of the poem.

'Anthem for Doomed Youth'

Written in September 1917, the poem is a requiem for the generation of young men who were slaughtered like cattle on the battlefields of France. It mingles in the formalities of the sonnet form, the sounds of the battle and the grief of those left behind to create an enduring statement of the horror and the pity of all war.

BEFORE YOU READ

- Study the many drafts of the poem in an attempt to identify the degree of effort which Owen put into the definition of its themes and in their technical expression.
- Read Yeats' 'The Wanderings of Oisin'.
- Read Laurence Binyon's 'For the Fallen', which Owen himself had read some two years before writing this poem. Consider the images of mourning presented by Binyon and the controlled tone in which he, too, depicts the grief of those who mourn for loved ones lost in battle.

YOUR FIRST RESPONSE

A CLOSER ANALYSIS

The commencing tone of the poem is confrontational – the rhetorical question of the first line is straight to the point about the manner in which the young men have met their death and the funeral rites performed in recognition of their passing. The answer is equally dramatic and matter of fact. What additional effect is gained by the commencement of line 2 with 'only' and by the qualification of the personified anger of the guns? Of the onomatopoeic report of the rifles' 'rapid rattle' which provide 'hasty orisons' for the dead?

Is there some suggestion here that the retort of the guns is in response to the voiced question of the first line? Does Owen bring the reader dramatically to the dangerous reality of the battlefield where one voiced question can lead to a dramatic fatal reply of gunfire?

The tone of the second stanza is, in its first two lines, serene by contrast to that of the first quatrain, echoing in its resigned catalogue of negatives the deathly unearthly silence following the fatal shooting of a soldier who dared to speak on the battlefield. Yet even this lull is brief. The rifle fire is soon followed by 'wailing' shells; choirs of insanity in strong contrast in their demented shrillness to the ordered, controlled expression of grief of the casualties' home shires expressed in bugle calls.

The fact of the soldiers' deaths clearly established in the octave, the poet in the sestet turns to the question of how the souls of the dead may be speeded to their destination as their bodies lie in their former homes (or where they fell on the field). Their goodbyes will not now be expressed by handshakes but by the last message of their eyes. Their pall shall be the paleness of their girls' brows; their funeral wreaths merely the tender quiet thoughts of those they leave behind; the final resignation to the loss of loved ones captured in the ritualistic gesture of the 'drawing-down of blinds'.

The techniques

Consider the contribution made to the development of the poem's ideas and subject matter by:
- the structural, tonal and thematic effect of the two rhetorical questions
- the contrast between the noise of gunfire (the 'monstrous anger' of the heavy artillery, the rifle fire and the overhead shells) and the noise of the bugle and the moments of silence (at the death of each soldier, and at home after the bugle call)
- the authenticity of the poem's evocation through alliteration, assonance and onomatopoeia of the noise of the battlefield
- the weighty heaviness and dull echoing sound of heavy artillery captured onomatopoeically in 'monstrous'
- the emphasis on eyes

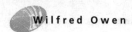

- the powerful dramatic effect achieved by simple words, such as 'sad shires' and 'slow dusk'
- the resonance brought to the poem by the repeated negatives

The themes

Consider the following thematic possibilities:

- the ignominy and ugliness of each individual soldier's death on the battlefield
- the contrast between the funeral rites of peacetime and the funeral rites of the battlefield
- the mockery made by the seeming superficiality of ritualised mourning of the profundity of suffering experienced by those who die on the battlefield and those who grieve at their loss
- the noise and ugliness of trench warfare
- the veneration of those women, mothers, girlfriends, wives, who lose their menfolk in war
- the incapacity of words to express the pain of final farewells to the slain

The universal elements

The poem has its genesis in Owen's first-hand experience of the horrors of the French battlefield but preserves for all time the ugliness and pain of death on the battlefield and the profundity of grief felt by those who are left behind.

YOUR SECOND RESPONSE

1. 'Anthem for Doomed Youth' is a popular inclusion in poetry anthologies. Does it merit this notoriety?
2. Owen reworked 'Anthem for Doomed Youth' a number of times before, by 25th September 1917, he was satisfied with the final version. Does its technical and thematic achievement evidence the poet's obvious effort?
3. 'There is a central paradox in 'Anthem for Doomed Youth' in that the poem derides the ineptitude of formal ceremony in acknowledging the suffering of those slain on the battlefield, when it is, itself, a very formal poem and successful in its use of poetic formalities.' Discuss.

'Dulce et Decorum Est'

Described by Owen as 'a gas poem', 'Dulce et Decorum Est' was subtitled 'To a Certain Poetess', a Miss Jessie Pope, whose verse celebrated popular patriotism. The title is taken from Horace's *Odes* meaning 'It is sweet and meet to die for one's country.'

BEFORE YOU READ

- Research the use of poisonous gas in World War I.
- Research the properties of chlorine and mustard gas which were used against the allied troops.
- See if you can locate copies of Miss Jessie Pope's verse and consider the popular romantic view of war espoused in them.

YOUR FIRST RESPONSE

A CLOSER ANALYSIS

The opening is dramatic, confronting the imagination not with images of heroes but images of decrepitude – their ugliness vocal as well as visual. Consider the power and physicality of the first phrase, it suggestion of tiredness and submission, and its extension by the simile. Is any greater drama added by the fact that these beggars are 'old' and 'knock-kneed'? What accounts for their difficult progress? Merely fatigue? Or the mud? Or the burden of despair?

NOTE

- the nature of the consonants which are alliterated: heavy, harsh sounding, laboured
- the effect of the use of 'cursed' as a definition of progress
- the weightiness of 'udge' in 'sludge' – and its onomatopoeic possibilities
- the assault on the nobility of the soldiers' individual identities by the reference to them as 'hags'
- the cumulative visual effect of 'beggars under sacks' and 'hags'

Their backs turned to the flare, the men trudge to their rest. What is the effect of these flares being 'haunting' and that rest being 'distant'? Are not the men caught in the middle of some kind of no-man's-land? Between the two worlds of fighting and of rest? Mud, lit by red flashes. What kind of landscape is this?

The first short sentence of line 5 create its own drama, especially in the matter-of-factness of its tone. The rhythm of the poem is slowed, brought almost to a standstill. The redness of the flares is then caught up again in the bloodied feet of the men. Their lameness and their blindness reiterate and extend the ideas of the first four lines. The men are 'drunk with fatigue' and deaf to the sound of the falling shells, onomatopoeically realised in 'hoots'. Even the shells are 'tired'. Is this not the weariest hell of literature?

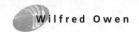

Line 9 breaks the metrical steadiness and the lethargy of the tone of the first stanza. Someone (perhaps Owen himself) finds sufficient strength to warn the others. What is the expectation as to the movement thus evoked, by the poet's choice of the word, 'ecstasy'? Is there not an irony in the use of such a pleasant word in such circumstances?

The progressive aspect of the verbs (the '-ing' endings) transport the reader into the midst of the ensuing confusion. One man did not respond quickly enough. He flounders 'like a man in fire or lime'. The image is a tactile as well as a visual recreation of a man fighting for life in the midst of mustard gas. He is cut off from those who can but watch him through the dim panes of their gas masks. The battlefield on which he dies has the colour and the movement of the sea. Is the man's 'drowning' therefore a silent visual performance? A surreal experience? The stuff of future nightmares?

Lines 15 and 16 are isolated as is the experience and consequence of the previous events they elaborate. The speaker is haunted by this particular death. The victim plunges at him in his dreams, his noisy suffocation onomatopoeically recreated. It is a nightmare in which time is suspended as the man's death is extended through a sequence of pain.

The dream of this drowning is as psychologically and emotionally 'smothering' as was the real event for the man who endured it and the spectators of the drama of his pain. This drama, and the enduring image of the death cart and of the final death throes of the barely living or newly dead devil thrown into it, are Gothic in the depth of their horror. Again the image recreated is as aural as it is visual – and horrifyingly tactile. The 'froth' of the 'corrupted lungs' hints at sea foam, the 'gargling' is that of the tide. The image is cancerous and bitter. Do the similes merely emphasise the point or elaborate on and develop it?

The reference to 'tongues' of line 24 is taken up in the 'tell' of the next line. Thus the admonishment delivered by the last four lines of the poem is given tactile definition. The Horatian tag is but an 'old Lie'. How obscene therefore is it for the reader to perpetuate it?

The techniques

Consider the contribution made to the development of the poem's ideas and subject matter by:
- the sustained imagery of mud, fatigue and confusion
- the irony of the title
- the extended metaphor of the battlefield as a surreal hell, and of the gassed man's world as a green sea
- sentence length and sentence placement
- the use of progressive aspect for verbs
- the harshness and heaviness of the sounds which dominate the tonal landscape of the poem

- the use of colour
- the devil and hellish imagery
- the surprise of the poem's conclusion

The themes

Consider the following thematic possibilities:

- the ugliness of the battlefield
- the surreal world of no-man's-land
- the peculiar suffering of death by mustard gas
- the enduring psychological and emotional scars of war
- the enormous gulf of understanding between those at home who promote war as a romantic, glorious exercise and dying for one's country as an act of nobility, and those who fight and die in war and know the true horror and ignominy and desecration of the individual on the battlefield

The universal elements

The poem is grounded in the particular horrors of trench warfare and mustard gas attacks of World War I, yet it captures, too, the horror of any battlefield, the ugliness of a soldier's death at the hands of unfeeling weaponry and the fatalistic despair felt by his companions who are unable to assist him but must carry the nightmare of his passing all their lives.

YOUR SECOND RESPONSE

1. Analyse the contribution made to the poem's meaning by the poet's choice of imagery and use of metre.
2. In 'Dulce e Decorum Est' has Owen defined the indefinable? Discuss the effectiveness of its elaboration of the enduring horrors of the battlefield.

'Miners'

Written in response to the Podmore Hall Colliery disaster of 12 January 1918 which killed both men and boy miners, the poem suggests by its title the occupations of many of the working men who had enlisted for war service. It also suggests in its irony the activities of the trench diggers and their journey into the depths of despair – even to hell. At the same time, it reminds the reader of the civilian life that is abandoned on the battlefield.

Most of all, it is a poem of protest which acknowledges the readiness with which future generations will ignore the sacrifices of those who gave their lives in order to preserve British civilisation and the British home.

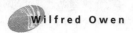

BEFORE YOU READ

- Research the history of the Podmore Hall Colliery disaster at Halmerend on 12 January 1918, in the newspapers of the time.
- Revise the nature and effect of pararhymes.
- Research trench construction on the battlefields of the Western Front.

YOUR FIRST RESPONSE

A CLOSER ANALYSIS

The poem begins deceptively with an image of domestic harmony and peaceful solitude. Yet it is a scene that is alive with the voice of the coal (onomatopoeically captured in 'whispering') and its personified wistfulness. What is the tone? Itself wistful? Reminiscing? Philosophical? Sad? Is the 'hearth' of line 1 also suggestive of the 'heart'? What is the effect of the pararhymes, 'hearth;' and 'earth'? An introduction of a sense of uneasiness? A suggestion of the co-existence of an elemental discordance with this primitive serenity of the home and hearth?

The second stanza is an imaginative journey back in time to that Earth of 'frond-forests' when time was slow and lives 'sly'. Is this world merely passively beautiful? Or is there a suggestion of malice existing and actively destroying life, even then. How powerful an image of death is that of the 'smothered ferns'? Is 'smothered' onomatopoeic? Are its sounds swallowed and muffled even as the act which is adjectivally delineated? Do the fawns suggest innocence? Vulnerability?

The beauty and innocence of the imagery of the second stanza is destroyed in the first two lines of the third. The 'steam-phantoms' are ghosts – from a past defined in an image of wickedness – Time's witches cauldron. This primeval world which might be evoked by the fire would predate the procreation of both birds and men. What extra force to these ideas is given by the simplicity of the imagery?

But the coals of this fire eschew these softer images and conjure instead the sound of moaning which accompanied their excavation. The images of boys and men are united by both the alliteration of 'wr' and the assonance of 'i'. Both are of disturbance and of suffering. The colliers have become soldiers, their tunnels, trenches. Suffocation in a collapsed mine parallels suffocation in a gas attack. Is it that the coals are determined to speak for those whose voices have been silenced and whose suffering the coal has observed first hand?

The fire conjures up images of bones. How more horrifying are they because of their contrast – the colour of the cinder-shard – and because of their numberlessness? Are these the two visual elements the poet has taken with him from the trenches? That memory of working closely and deliberately with the bones of the dead? What is the coal which has 'charred' the hearts of many? Is it the mud of Flanders' battlefields? Why do so few of those who have experienced its horrors remember them? Is it that most try to forget the nightmare?

The coal and its murmuring calls up from the depths of the speaker's memory, the trench diggers of the Western Front, digging their own pits and dying in them, the lies of peace repudiated by their deaths.

Time after battlefield sorrows is personified in the lives of those whose comfort has been assured by the sacrifice of the men in the pits. The miner and the soldier images conjoin in individual acts of sacrifice guaranteeing the pleasant aging of others beside the embers their lives have provided (either actually or metaphorically).

The sacrifice of the miner and of the soldier will guarantee prosperity for centuries to come for those who will not remember those who were lost in coal mine or battlefield mud.

NOTE
* the emphasis on the comfortable lives of those who reap the benefit of the soldiers' and miners' sacrifice
* the definition of the nature and the extent of that suffering through the load imagery
* the contrast of sound and conjured meaning between 'groaned' and 'crooned'
* the easy sleep of the comfortable – in contrast to the 'wry sleep 'of the miners (line 15)
* the simplicity and the poignancy and the acknowledged camaraderie born out of the joint experience of suffering in the phrase 'us poor lads'
* the understated horror of the final line of the poem

The final statement is one of subdued criticism. What is its tone? Fatalistic? Accepting? Hurt? Grieving? Disappointment? Resignation to the selfishness of society? To the brevity of glory? To the shortness of the public memory?

The techniques

Consider the contribution made to the development of the poem's ideas and subject matter by:
* the sustained imagery of fire and coal
* the ironic ambiguity of the title
* the extended metaphor of the mine as a battlefield trench
* the use of pararhymes
* the use of onomatopoeia
* the graphic nature of the imagery in defining the deaths of men and boys and in defining what each leaves behind in dying

- the use of colour
- the devil and hellish imagery
- the surprise – and subdued bitterness – of the poem's conclusion

The themes

Consider the following thematic possibilities:
- the power and meaning of the domestic fireside
- the special relationship between humankind and fire
- the sacrifices which ensure the continuity of existence
- the indifference of society to – and its incapacity to comprehend – the reality of suffering upon which its comforts are founded
- the readiness of future generations to forget the sacrifices of those who have given their lives in war in order to preserve their way of life
- the lie that is patriotism
- the lack of nobility of death in the (mine or battlefield) pit

The universal elements

The poem brings to account the indifference of each member of society whose homely comforts are guaranteed by the sacrifice of others – commoner or soldier, it does not really matter.

YOUR SECOND RESPONSE

How masterfully does Owen balance the dual central imagery of 'Miners'? Does his poem celebrate the indifference or the gratitude of society to the sacrifice of both the soldier and the miner?

'Insensibility'

Written in March 1918, the poem is the poet's own litany of the battlefield horrors – of experience which denies the beauty and the hopefulness of the Beatitudes. In it he categorises those who have the particular blessing of a refined indifference to the horrors of war. For any poet, this indifference is to be celebrated for it allows the poet to preserve his objectivity to events and scenes which would otherwise drive him into the grotesque reality of nightmare.

BEFORE YOU READ
- Read the Beatitudes in the Bible (Matthew v:3–11)
- Research the place of Beaumont Hamel in World War I confrontation.

A CLOSER ANALYSIS

Happy are those who:

- become dehumanised – living corpses – before they are actually meet death
- are without the compassion which troubles those who walk on the corpses of their fellows
- who are wiped out in the front line

CONSIDER

- the physical strength of the images of lines 1 to 4.
- the rejection of romantic description of soldiers' deaths – they are men not flowers
- the objective ugliness of the gaps which signify individual deaths
- the 'l' alliteration which stresses the numbers of those killed – and then the dismissal of concern at the statistics of such fatalities

Some who achieve the indifference to the suffering and deaths of others of Part I also lose their capacity to feel for themselves. What is their motivation in achieving such objectivity to their physical and personal reality? The solution it brings to their fear of death, and to this grim statistics which bring with it the promise of their own demise?

Happy are those who have lost their imaginations:

- they can then devote all their emotional and physical energy to the practical matter of carrying their ammunition and their pack; and their wounds ache only as physical rather than psychological ailments
- blood and wounds have lost their capacity to shock and to hurt the spirit
- they can laugh among the dying; their sensitivities numbed, their hearts inactivated, their feelings cauterised in battle fire

How effective is the poet's choice of colour in Part III? The consciousness of wounds? The imagery of cauterisation?

Happy is the soldier home who:

- has no notion of attacks proceeding on the field – nor of the fatalities such attacks will inevitably bring

Happy is the lad who was never trained, and who can therefore sing as those with the experience of the realities of war, march in the realisation that they march not only into dusk but towards the larger night of Death. How effective are the contrasts here between knowledge and lack of knowledge?

What is the meaning and point of the rhetoric of Part V? That the untutored indifference of the eyes of the boy is the point of view which all should adopt, even the returning soldiers? Is this the means of subduing the memories of bloody deaths? Does this boy also define the best view to adopt of the enemy? A human being whose life – and death – will not amount to much?

Part VI shocks with its reversal. The blessings celebrated in Parts I to V are naught but curses. After all, 'dullards' cannot share in the universal grief and pity of war. How is the message of this part strengthened by the poet's use of alliter-ation and assonance? How dramatic is the imagery? How moving the special feelings enunciated as the 'whatevers' to which such 'wretched' unfeeling men are immune.

The techniques

Consider the contribution made to the development of the poem's ideas and subject matter by:
* the imagery of blood, darkness and battle
* the irony of the title (Is not the poem a plea for sensibility?)
* the emphasis on the physical body of individual man – this, after all, is the subject of the unfeeling, neutral statistics of battlefield casualties
* the use of quatrosyllabic words to define the sensibilities at the heart of the poem
* the graphic nature of the battlefield imagery
* the use of colour and contrast
* the surprise of the poem's conclusion

The themes

Consider the following thematic possibilities:
* the shocking reality and terrifying statistics of battlefield fatalities
* the psychological and emotional burden of battlefield experience
* the indelible images of blood and corpses carried by all soldiers who have expe-rienced the war
* the gulf of understanding between those who cheer men on to their deaths in hometown parades and those who know the reality of war
* the fight for the battle scarred soldier to hold onto his capacity for pity and grief – and thereby his essential humanity ; without these sensibilities war has killed him even if he has escaped death on the front line

The universal elements

'Insensibility' ironically exemplifies the value of and need for preservation of sensibility in the face of the horrifying casualty statistics and conditions of warfare. Only this can preserve our essential humanity.

1. '"Insensibility" ennobles the opposite.' What insights into the human cost of war are provided by this poem?
2. In 'Insensibility', Owen provides the world with the beatitudes of war. What promises of salvation do they offer? To whom?

'The Show'

Written in 1918, 'The Show' is a dramatic, theatrical statement of the full horror of the battlefield, employing an extended metaphor of the battlefield as the maggot-infested face of a gigantic corpse to capture the complete immersion of the soldier in the surrealistic, yet personal, nightmare of his own death.

BEFORE YOU READ

• Read William Butler Yeats' 'The Shadowy Waters'.
• Read Thomas Hardy's *The Dynasts*, and note particularly the use pattern of imagery used in this novel.
• Read Henri Barbusse's novel *Under Fire* (translated from the French).
• Research drawings and photographs of the French battlefields of World War I.

A CLOSER ANALYSIS

The lines from Yeats are the words of gods looking down on the earth from the heights of heavens. Owen's poem catalogues the horrible pantomime of death which gives the souls of the dead soldier their perspective.

The first line of the poem is almost serene in tone, as the persona speaks with a certain numbness of his position as the companion of Death, hovering at a 'vague height' above the battlefield. Note the confusion captured in 'un-remembering' and the 'how' and 'why' of the words of line 2.

How suitable an introduction to horror is the description of the battlefield as 'a sad land'? Does this phrase capture in its simplicity the poet's full moral condemnation of the speaker's world of war? Or is it in its simplicity, a deceptive overture to the horrors which are yet to be presented?

The land is caught in a fever of decay. How more awful is the woe because of its hollowness? How seriously is this hollowness realised? How effective is the

alliteration and its combination with images of pocks and scabs in capturing the disgust of the vision? The portrait of the battlefield's face begins with its sweating brow. Are the grey craters its lifeless eyes? And the pocks and scabs its blasted cheeks?

The barbed wire moves across the beard of the battlefield in grim mockery of the beards of the men who attempt to circumnavigate it, moving in lines like 'thin caterpillars, slowly uncoiled'. The image is that of maggots slowly writhing across the face of a corpse, luxuriating in a private world of decay.

Each maggot-like creature seemed to push itself like a plug into the trenches – only to writhe and die there. How is the ugliness of such deaths captured in the cumulative effect of 'writhed and shrivelled' and the delay before the creatures are at last stilled by death – 'killed'?

The mounds of earth thrown up by the impact of shells and thrown up by the trench diggers form their own wart-like, hilly topography, each mound given prominence by a collar of 'slimy paths'. What contribution to the ugliness of this imagery is made by the discordant minor key of the sounds of 'trailed' and 'scraped'? What insight into the sounds of the battlefield as well as its sights?

What is the effect of the repetition of the disappearance of the battlefield creatures down holes? Is their leaving of the dawn for the darkness of the holes an allegorical enactment of the soldiers' desertion of life for death? Are the holes also the nasal openings of the battlefield face? Is it the smell of rotting corpses and of gangrenous wounds which emanates from them? Are these the sources of the foul vapours that come from these openings?

Undeterred by the stinking mire into which they are marching, soldiers wearing the brown British uniforms make their way intently, if 'on dithering feet', towards the strings of grey-uniformed Germans, their weaponry held high like spines. What is the import of the porcupine image? Is it, too, English? What is the effect of the contrast between this mire and the green fields that the soldiers eschew for the battlefield mud?

The grey strings have the advantage of numbers, yet are also eaten. The death throes of the combatants are reported matter-of-factly, each action evidencing suffering delineated carefully from their final stillness in death. What is achieved by the repetition of the account? An acknowledgment of the equal suffering of casualties on both sides? A recounting of terrible deaths in slow motion?

The grotesqueness of these death throes shocks the observer/speaker out of his indifference, and pulls him back to earth, 'like a feather'.

Death falls with him – but not in silence – his descent is accompanied by 'a deepening moan'.

Yet, in the midst of the mire, Death becomes the guide to his companion, pointing worm-like to the feet of the dead corpse, feet which could have belonged to any individual in the strings of men who fell upon each other. His show is complete, however, when he points as his finale to the 'fresh-severed head' of his companion, the poem's persona. This final image both shocks and terrifies, notwithstanding the poem's detailed exploration of ugliness and death on the battlefield. Why is this so? Is it because this is an individual fate which the reader now confronts rather than the numerous fates of whole lines of men? And because it is the fate of an individual who, in the course of the poem, the reader has come to accept as a companion reporter – and who has been lulled with the victim by the act of reporting into believing that this man is to be but an observer rather than a fated participant in the grotesque events of this war?

The techniques

Consider the contribution made to the development of the poem's ideas and subject matter by:
- the sustained imagery of festering decay
- the pun of the title (picture show and battle)
- the extended metaphor of the battlefield as one giant maggot-ridden face, and the associated metaphors used to define the two sides fighting across its land-scape and the slime-filled trenches which gave it form
- the ascription of each sentence to a separate stanza
- the variety of rhyme
- the harshness of the sounds which dominate the tonal landscape of the poem
- the use of colour (British khaki and German grey)
- the sense of height
- the shock of the poem's conclusion

The themes

Consider the following thematic possibilities:
- the ugly brutality of war which drowns all combatants in its mire
- the shock of death
- an officer's duty to lead his men to safety
- the chaos and confusion of the battlefield
- the ugliness and stench of corpses
- the irrelevance in battle of the colour of your uniform other than to specify those whom you fight and those with whom you die
- the universal horror and suffering endured by all soldiers
- the determination of men to fight notwithstanding the danger
- the triumph of death in the 'theatre' of war (note the poem's title)

The universal elements

Owen expresses in ' The Show' the emotional, physical, spiritual and moral horror of war as deftly as he captures the stench and the ugliness and the physical reality of the battlefield.

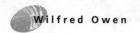

YOUR SECOND RESPONSE

1. 'In "The Show", the politics of war are forgotten in a celebration of its horror and ugliness.' Discuss.
2. How effective is the imagery of 'The Show'? Does its depiction of the horrors of war have any relevance beyond the trench warfare of World War I?

'The Send-Off'

'The Send-Off' confronts the political and social hypocrisy with which men are sent to their almost certain deaths on the battlefield. Its bitter irony draws heavily on the delusions of glory with which their suffering was officially whitewashed.

BEFORE YOU READ

* Conduct your own research on the enlistment of troops in World War I and on the conduct of their marches off to war.
* View a film of World War I troop embarkation.

A CLOSER ANALYSIS

The length of the first line imitates the length of the column of soldiers marching (perhaps only half unwittingly) to the battlefield and to their deaths. Why do the men sing? Is the bravado suggested by their singing genuine or pretended? Are the 'darkening lanes' ominous? Is the atmosphere they create full of foreboding? Of the intimation of death?

How surprising is the speaker's use of 'gay'? How qualified is it by the choice of adjective? How does the alliteration dramatise the qualification?

How dramatic is the image of lines 4 and 5? Is the sense of foreboding suggested in the previous lines quantified by it? Is the image dramatised by its isolation from the previous and following lines of the poem?

The porters who watch the men go are 'dull'. Is it that they have seen so many pass before them never to return? Or is theirs the indifference of the uncaring? By contrast, the tramp will miss them. Is it the loss of their friendship which he regrets? Has he had the opportunity to get to know these men as individuals whereas they are anonymous faces to the porter?

The departure is without note or fanfare, marked merely by a lamp 'winked to the guard'. Why the lack of ceremony? The sense of surreptitiousness?

Why the secrecy, the hushed send-off? What revelation of reason is contained in the simile? If these men did not belong to the speaker's regiment, to whom did they belong? Did war engulf them, swallow up their identities, even before they reached the Front?

Nor is it known by the speaker whether these men mocked the flowers given to them by the women.

What is known about them? That they will not return in triumph? That they will number on return too few for grand fanfare? That those who will return will 'creep back' – and even then to anonymity. Why no songs of praise? Why such absence of recognition at their departure and upon their return?

The techniques

Consider the contribution made to the development of the poem's ideas and subject matter by:
- the imagery
- the use of colour
- the alternating three and two line stanzas
- the use of traditional symbols associated with soldiers and war: wreaths and flowers
- the impact of individual words
- use of rhyme which creates a deceptive air of simplicity and an atmosphere of innocence in the dramatisation of an event, the tragic consequences of which are hidden in a conspiracy of official hypocrisy

The themes

Consider the following thematic possibilities:
- the grim fate awaiting many of those who dare to march off to war
- the lack of meaning in the soldiers' farewells
- the loss of personal identity in war
- the official secretive processing of the cannon fodder
- society's indifference to the soldiers' sacrifice

The universal elements

'The Send-Off' dramatises the political and social hypocrisy which accompanies the sacrifice of individuals in war.

YOUR SECOND RESPONSE

1. '"The Send-Off" demonstrates Owen's capacity to deal with the most horrifying ideas in the simplest manner.' Do you agree with this assessment of the poem?

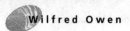

2. Write an analysis of 'The Send-Off'. How effectively does this poem embody Owen's protest at the pointless and unacknowledged waste of human life in war?

'Futility'

Published in June 1918 in *The Nation*, this gently haunting poem portrays personal loss through its depiction of a universal scene which has the simplicity of a visual parable.

BEFORE YOU READ

• Research the social origins of the soldiers who fought on the battlefields of France.
• Research the history of the sun as a poetic symbol.

YOUR FIRST RESPONSE

A CLOSER ANALYSIS

The poem opens with a helpful suggestion – from a bystander who observes the desperate attempt of his comrades to revive one of their own. What is its tone? Desperate? Perplexed? Gentle? Coaxing?

The simplicity of the suggestion is filled out by the explanation as to why it was made: once back at home the sun had awoken the victim – and even in France – at least until this snow. What is the effect of the metaphor of ' snow'? Does it domesticate the rain of bullets which felled the victim? Indicate a desire on the part of the speaker to avoid the grim reality of his battlefield world? Enunciate a subconscious desire for home?

Is this the voice of innocent youth?

The imaginative compass of the speaker is transported home in the sestet. His logic becomes more urgent. After all, are not the seeds and was not the earth itself awoken by the sun?

Line 10 increases this urgency. The limbs which now lay so low were dear achieved – and the sides are still warm. The early confidence gives way to questioning.

The tone of the speaker becomes more strident as he searches for a reason, for some explanation and understanding of the death of his companion. His focus and the imagery extend beyond the immediate to the universal. Finding no answer, he questions the integrity and point of all existence. If youth is reared to be killed in this war, was there any point in the pattern of evolution which facilitated his birth?

The techniques

Consider the contribution made to the development of the poem's ideas and subject matter by:

- the poet's use of the sonnet form, and in particular the contrast between the octave and sestet
- the sun (life) symbolism in contrast to the snow (death) symbolism
- the use of rhetoric
- the full rhyme of 'snow' and 'know' and the pararhyme of 'know' and 'now', and the assonance established between 'know', 'snow' and 'unsown'. Is it to suggest in the sounds of the poem the perplexity of the youthful speaker at the ease by which the life of his companion has been taken?
- the pattern of imagery: 'fields' linking to 'clay'; 'snow' linking to the sunless earth of before the beginnings of life

The themes

Consider the following thematic possibilities:

- the pity and perplexity of war
- the inability of the soldier on the field to rationalise the death which he encounters every day
- the simple rural origins of many of the combatants
- the innocence of youth and the wastefulness of its sacrifice in war
- the helplessness of all humankind in the face of death

The universal elements

This poem personalises death in war; its speaker speaks for all who question the value of patriotism and the sacrifice of young lives to its service.

YOUR SECOND RESPONSE

1. '"Futility" demonstrates the greater impact of the description of the death of one man rather than the reporting of deaths of multitudes.' Do you agree? How effective is this poem as a statement of the waste of human life in war?
2. Simple language and traditional ideas can be given new life in poetry. What is Owen's achievement in 'Futility'?
3. Is 'Futility' too short and too simple a poem to warrant much critical attention?

'Mental Cases'

This is a strong poem with an arresting title, drawing the reader immediately into the psychological, spiritual and emotional devastation of war.

BEFORE YOUR READ

Research the nature and effects of shell shock suffered by so many soldiers in World War I.

YOUR FIRST RESPONSE

A CLOSER ANALYSIS

The mental patients prompt a rhetoric of horror and disbelief.

Is there not an immediate pathos in the fact that their identities are not known? Is this the point of the first question with which the poem opens? Or is its initial emphasis on the patients' alienation and isolation from the everyday world?

Does the dramatic image of 'purgatorial shadows' prepare the reader for the physical ugliness and oddity of behaviour catalogued in lines 3 and 4? What is the cumulative effect of the imagery? Living skeletons? Living death?

The patients' eyes are 'gouged' with pain, their sockets 'fretted' – their pain is inescapable even to the most indifferent of observers. The physical evidence of it is incontestable.

Their hair is wet with sweat; so too are their palms. So ugly and wracked are their forms that they question the very reality of the observer. Surely, this is hell.

The explanation is simple – yet even more horrifying in its details than the present physical decrepitude of the patients. These men:

- have been psychologically 'ravished' by death. Is the image of rape effective and appropriate?
- have been witnesses to multitudinous murders. Memory has ineluctably massaged the images of each murder into their scalps.
- have wandered (and still in their mind's eye) wander over 'sloughs' of corpses, their tread squeezing blood from lungs which once respired in laughter
- cannot even now escape the incessant sound of the guns and the compelling sight of human muscles torn from bodies by their shellfire
- have known human 'carnage' and the squandering of life on an unrivalled scale

So deeply etched are all these horrors into each individual patients' conscious-ness that they are beyond the reach of medicine.

This being the case, the patients eschew the sunlight as, in its brightness, it reminds them of the smear of blood. Night's blackness also becomes the blackness of blood. Dawn is but mimicry of an opening wound.

Thus the patients present as hideous, comical corpses. And thus they pluck at each other – and more particularly at those who tend them as representatives of the politicians who gave them ' war and madness'.

What is the effect of the logical progression of the poem? Its conversational mode? Is it to bring form to the formless horror of war which each patient rep-resents? Is it to objectify the tone with which these horrors are enumerated, to prevent their reality from being drowned in sensationalism and emotive lan-guage? Is it to suspend the listener's and reader's shock long enough to enable the total reality of the battlefield to be defined? Does it suspend the reader's response indefinitely?

The techniques

Consider the contribution made to the development of the poem's ideas and subject matter by:

- the dialogue mode which forms the basis structure of the poem
- the compilation of interrogatives which form the first stanza. Is the interrogator struggling to deal with the complexities of the images of suffering before him?
- the emphasis on the visual, tactile and auditory horror of the battlefield
- the multiplicity of blood imagery
- the capitalisation of the Dead

The themes

Consider the following thematic possibilities:

- the grotesque reality of the battlefield and unquantifiable suffering meted out to soldier combatants who enter its world
- the ignorance and indifference with which politicians condemn others to die
- the enduring nightmare of battlefield horrors brought home by the survivors of war
- the gulf of understanding between those who have remained at home and those whose legacy of suffering they observe and cannot explain for themselves

The universal elements

'Mental Cases' defines the enduring horror of war for all combatants and the inescapable nightmare into which memory plunges some of them, even on their return home.

YOUR SECOND RESPONSE

1. Has Owen overdone the imagery of blood and horror in 'Mental Cases'? Does it suffer from sensationalism despite its logical structure?

2. What contribution to your understanding of the battlefield and the effects of war is provided by Owen's depiction of some of its survivors in this poem?

'Strange Meeting'

Frequently chosen in anthologies as a seminal statement on the mutuality of suffering endured by the universal soldier, 'Strange Meeting' is a vision poem which represents much of what is enduring and best in Owen's work.

BEFORE YOU READ

- Read John Keats' 'The Fall of Hyperion' and note particularly the significance in that poem of the poet's sighting of the face of Moneta.
- Read Luke xxii: 44 in the New Testament of the Bible.
- Read Shelley's *Prometheus Unbound I*, 564–5.

YOUR FIRST RESPONSE

A CLOSER ANALYSIS

The first three lines of the poem suggests the speaker's escape to a world of timeless fantasy. How effective is the enjambment in suggesting the ease and swiftness with which he travelled, seemingly through space and time?

What contribution to the atmosphere is made by the use of 'profound' and 'titanic'? What dramatic intensity do they give to the nouns which each of these adjectives qualifies? What sense of physical effort is captured in the verbs and, in particular, in the effect of their individual sounds?

The fourth line begins with a qualification yet is linked to the previous statement by the pararhyme of lines 3 and 4. Is this to emphasise the fact that the speaker's experience is not singular but rather universal? The sleepers are 'encumbered', a weighty word to describe a weighty state of being – out of reach of the speaker and of all the rest of humanity.

'Probed' suggests an affront, an act of strong aggression – and it is to this act on the speaker's part that one of the speakers is stirred. His reaction to his prober is paradoxical – an act of blessing which is in truth an act of fear. Why then did he smile? Was it in friendly recognition of his companion? Or as an expression of a certain sense of satisfaction that at last his killer has met the same fate as that he dealt out to him?

NOTE

- the discordance of the pararhymes of lines 9 and 10 – and the feeling of unease which is underscored by their use
- the impact of the repetition of 'I knew' – its dramatisation of the awfulness of the awareness of the truth of his situation which dawns on the speaker.
- the re-visualisation – and re-enactment – of the moment of the sleeping soldier's death

The face of the awakened man demands the particular attention of the speaker. Why? Is it the depth and breadth of suffering ingrained there? Its representative quality? Is the speaker's surprise at its visual expression of horror surprising? Naive? Simplistic? Unthinking? Or is it indicative of the speaker's own relief at having escaped the noise of the battlefield made by both the guns and the men they wounded? The dialogue between the two men reveals:

- the hopelessness and the wasted lives of those killed in war
- the lost loves, the lost beauty, the lost joys and the lost griefs of existence hunted fervently in youth
- the lost opportunities to make others laugh; the lost contribution to others' mourning which could have been made by the tears of those too soon killed
- the loss of the truth which each could have told – of the pity of war and the pity distilled by war

Now, humankind will either content itself with what this war has spoiled, or discontent itself and so involve itself in yet another war. How effective is the pararhyme of lines 26 and 27 in emphasising the futility and pointlessness of these two equally unsatisfactory options for the future of humankind? Why will humanity move so swiftly to destroy itself? Is it that only the dead have gained the self-awareness needed to bring a halt to the history of humankind's self-destruction? Is it only the dead who would speak out? Why will none alive 'break ranks'? What is implied here? The social endorsement of the cycle of destruction that is humankind's perennial commitment to war? Criticism of the punishment wreaked out to those who speak out against the war?

The speaker sums up all that has been lost to the world by his death – his unique identity. How do the pararhymes of lines 30 and 31 capture and dramatise his personal value?

How much has he missed? What is the significance of that which he has lost? Of his lost contribution? Is there a Christ metaphor in the image of his lost ablutions? An echo of Christ's washing the feet of his disciples?

Here was a man who would have given his all – but not in the cesspool of war. The bloody wounds of conflict become but a metaphor for the self

sacrifice he would have been prepared to make for the betterment of his world, in order to achieve the greater self-knowledge of humankind and its awareness of the ultimate truths of existence.

Spaced dramatically apart from the speaker's previous rhetoric is his final admission – he is the enemy whom the speaker killed. His death is fresh – only yesterday did he die at the hands of the man he now confronts in hell. What kind of death is captured in the verbs by which his opponent's fatal actions and his response are defined? What feeling accompanies his final words? A sense of fatalism? Of acceptance of the inevitability of his own and his companion's fate given humankind's propensity throughout history to destroy itself?

The techniques

Consider the contribution made to the development of the poem's ideas and subject matter by:
- the use of parahyme
- the careful selection of verbs and the dramatic definition of individual and humankind's actions which is achieved by such selectivity
- the use of words suggesting ancient times
- the conjuring of pain
- the use of onomatopoeia in lines 4 and 13
- the use of dialogue to create a face to face confrontation of two enemies in death as they had confronted each other in life)
- the dramatic intensity given to the expression of abstract thought by the use of repetition in lines 15 and 16, 17 and 18, 19 and 36, and 25.
- tactile and visual imagery
- the use of metaphor

The themes

Consider the following thematic possibilities:
- the human propensity for war since primeval times
- the pointless sacrifice of youth in war
- the loss of potential for personal and social good, for courage and mastery of life in the death of any individual soldier
- the reluctant involvement of many soldiers in the cess of World War I
- the pointlessness of the soldiers' sacrifice, as nations will never criticise the havoc they created or shun future wars as a response to it

The universal elements

'Strange Meeting' is a universal statement of the pointlessness of the destruction of young men in war in the service of their country. It defines what each individual himself loses and what society loses as a result of his sacrifice to the ancient bloodlust of nations.

1. How effective a protest against war is 'Strange Meeting?'
2. '"Strange Meeting" exploits the traditional association of war and hell to make a special comment on the uselessness and waste and pity of war.' Analyse the achievement of this poem, using this statement as a starting point.

'The Sentry'

Written in the summer of 1918, 'The Sentry' plots the recurrent nightmares of battle which plague the returned soldier.

BEFORE YOU READ

- Investigate the details of trench warfare in World War I.
- Research the nature of the artillery used by both sides in World War I.

YOUR FIRST RESPONSE

A CLOSER ANALYSIS

The old Boche dug-out entombs the allied soldiers who find it in a murky atmosphere of stale air. The mud bars their escape. How complete a sensory definition of their experience is captured in the first ten lines of the poem? What tactile, auditory and olfactory images are portrayed in these lines?

How do rhythm and onomatopoeia work together in the first phrase of line 1? How onomatopoeic is 'slush' and 'whizz-bangs'? Is the reference to corpses in line 10 an anticlimax given the nature of the conditions and the events described in the previous lines?

What is the effect of the use of 'Boche'? Does it dehumanise the enemy? Particularise him? Reflect in the ugliness of the word, the ugliness of the enemy's character?

What is the impact of 'herded'? How well does it delineate the sheltering men's position? Is it not an extension of the cattle for slaughter metaphor which recurs in Owen's poems?

The whizz-bang which succeeds in entering the dug out is curiously animated with a seeming determination to seek out its victims. Its entry is dramatised onomatopoeically, each aspect of its progress particularised.

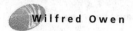

Is its 'snuffing the candles' full of symbolic promise of its capacity to snuff out the men's lives?

The whizz–bang brought with it muck and the sentry's body. Is the fact that this body has a voice a surprise? What is the tone of his complaint? Desperate? A gathering sense of doom? What contribution to the poem's atmosphere and theme is made by the assonance of 'ine' in the sentry's whining statement of his blindness? What compassion – and unspoken controlled desperation – is in the speaker's 'coaxing'? And what degree of hope in the elements of the test of the permanency of the sentry's blindness carried out by the speaker?

The sentry sobs as he cannot see even the 'least blurred light'. The image of his distended, bulging blind eyes haunt the speaker a long time after his anguished recognition of his fate. What contribution does the simile make to the evocation of the reality of both the sentry's nightmare and his companion's? What physicality does it bring to the description? What sense of colour? Of tactile sensation?

The speaker soon forgets the injured man as he goes about the business of war, posting the sentry's replacement and sending a scout to locate a stretcher, and 'floundering' himself to other posts in the 'shrieking air'. Are the shrieks simply those of the shells? Or are they also the shrieks of the men they maim and kill?

The fate of one man is soon submerged in the fates of many. How effective is the choice of 'wretches' to describe them? And how effective and accurate the verbs which define their fates? How ugly? How strongly visual, aural, olfactory and tactile?

The horror recedes into the past and the speaker puts his energy into forgetting them. Yet – one horror refuses to lie submerged in his unconscious – the plaintive voice of the blinded sentry as, his singular horror having been renewed by each fall of shells, he cried out that he could see their lights – long after they had died out.

NOTE

- the limited attention given by the speaker to the wounded man's continuing suffering
- the onomatopoeic effect of 'chattering'
- the onomatopoeic effect of 'crumps' and 'pummelled', by which the sounds of the shellfire obtain their own special reality as participants in the events of the poem
- the intensity of sound captured in the alliteration of 'dense din' and in the dramatic concentration of stress of the monosyllables
- the swift destruction by the second statement of the last line of the poem of the short-lived hope of the sentry expressed in the first half of that line

The techniques

Consider the contribution made to the development of the poem's ideas and subject matter by:

- the widespread use of onomatopoeia
- the selective use of verbs
- the use of proper nouns in lines 1, 16 and 24
- powerful metaphors in lines 4 and 9
- strongly literal simile in line 22
- the personification of the intrusive 'whizz-bang'
- the powerful and dramatic simplicity of monosyllables in lines 29 and 30, and line 35

The themes

Consider the following thematic possibilities:

- the peculiar horrors of trench warfare
- the insignificance of the suffering of the individual soldier in the hellish landscape of the battlefield
- the noise, and blood and mud and stench of the Front Line
- special pain and suffering inflicted by whiz-bangs
- the necessary pragmatism required of officers
- the enduring psychological and emotional scars of battlefield experience
- the desperate hopes of the wounded

The universal elements

The poem celebrates the individual pain of a sentry blinded on the battlefield and of the officer who could do nothing for him. It represents, however, the pain and suffering and despair felt by all casualties of war and the necessary – yet ultimately self-destructive – pragmatism required of those who must command men in war.

YOUR SECOND RESPONSE

1. Analyse the techniques used effectively by Wilfred Owen in 'The Sentry' to evoke the realities of the battlefield.
2. Is the message of 'The Sentry' limited to the trench warfare of World War I?
3. 'War is hell.' Use this statement as a starting point for your analysis of 'The Sentry'.
4. Is the title of Owen's poem 'The Sentry' justified?

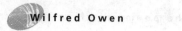

'Smile, smile, smile'

Written in September 1918, this poem is one of Owen's last. It parodies the optimism expressed in the popular song of the same title sung by troops and decries the demand of the politicians for total victory.

BEFORE YOU READ

*   Research all the verses of the troop song, 'Smile, smile, smile'.
*   Read Clemenceau's speech to the Senate published in *The Times*, 19 September 1918.

YOUR FIRST RESPONSE

A CLOSER ANALYSIS

The poem opens with a graphic picture of the decrepitude brought to young men by their experience of war. Their heads are limp, their eyes sunken. There is an implied irony in the fact that those who have suffered so much and known the dreadful other reality of the battlefield should now engage in such an innocuous civilian activity as reading the newspaper. Can they, however, ever rejoin the ranks of those whose only knowledge of and encounter with war is doing just this?

The satire of the print size is obvious. The dead are accorded much less notoriety than the plunder and pillage of war. Obvious too is the irony of the headline, 'Cheap Homes'. How many, however, will return to claim them?

Yet these homes must wait as the country's resources must be newly committed – to the construction of aerodromes. Of this the writer of the article is certain. This war has 'but begun'. Peace is to be shunned as an ignominy, an insult to those already consumed by the conflagration. Only those who have fought are deserving of the greatest glory. They have served the nation.

Why do the readers wonder at the journalist's use of 'nation'? What is the nature of their wonderment? Anger? Surprise? Bemusement? Silent, unspoken recognition of its meaninglessness? Of the idiocy of the rhetoric given the high casualty rate of those large numbers of Englishmen who took up the challenge on behalf of France?

How dramatic is the acknowledgment of the fact that these readers are amputees?

How inapt and how lacking in understanding is the response of those who view their smiles reported in the newspapers of their time? Is the experience of those who have fought and returned home maimed in spirit if not also in body beyond the understanding of those who belong only to the civilian world where war and its casualties are but the stuff of newspaper articles? Will cheap homes ever re-assimilate the returnees into this civilian world?

The techniques

Consider the contribution made to the development of the poem's ideas and subject matter by:

- irony and satire
- capitalisation
- the use of newspaper dialogue
- the use of rhyme, especially the swift movement from 'homes' to 'aerodromes' in lines 6 and 7.
- the distant rhetoric of the speech quoted in the newspaper article in contrast to the silent unspoken rhetoric of the soldiers
- the not so subtle details of the returnees' physical (and implied) mental condition

The themes

Consider the following thematic possibilities:

- the unbridgeable gulf between the nation of returned soldiers and the nation of civilians who have never known the horrors of the battlefield
- the special bond forged between returnees by their mutual experience of war
- the lies of war-time propaganda espoused by politicians in an attempt to feed the war machine
- the hollowness of victory
- the empty insincerity and unreality of the rhetoric spoken by leaders from the safety of their seats of power as they justify the sacrifice of others in the service of their nation

The universal elements

'Smile, smile, smile' defines, in the simple drama of soldiers reading civilian newspapers, the unbridgeable gulf of understanding which exists between those who have known the horrors of war and those who only read about it or who promote it. It also damns, in few words, the empty rhetoric of politicians who sacrifice their country's human and material resources to the service of hollow ideals.

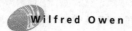

YOUR SECOND RESPONSE

1. What different view of war is presented by Owen in 'Smile, smile, smile'?
2. What divisions of experience and sincerity are portrayed in 'Smile, smile, smile'? How universal is its message?

'Spring Offensive'

The first draft of this poem was written by Owen in late September 1918. He did not live to complete his final revision of it.

The poem is written from Owen's experience of the Allied spring offensive in 1917 during which he was a member of the party which captured the French village of Fayet. The campaign lasted 12 days and Owen and many others who survived it emerged from the experience with shell shock.

BEFORE YOU READ

• Research the Allied campaign against the village of Fayet.
• Research battlefield conditions on the Front.
• Investigate the effects of shell shock.

YOUR FIRST RESPONSE

A CLOSER ANALYSIS

The poem places the reader in the midst of an action, when the men have gained a strategic position on a ridge. Some rest there. Why do others stand to stare into the sky beyond? Do they search for a pathway to eternity? Do they seek God? Do they sense their own impending deaths?

Is the blankness of the sky worrying? Challenging? Does it suggest an absence of meaning? Of answers? An absence of God?

Stanza 2 describes a summer reverie. Is there a special significance in the fact that it takes place on a battlefield? In the poet's emphasis on the men's bodies and on the sense of life which was flowing at that moment through their veins? What is the point of the simile? An emphasis on the fact that these bodies (and spirits) are wearied by war? Do the sky and its light confer with the wind and the grass to present an experience akin to death – a loss of consciousness of being?

Time drags as the men look back to the fields of buttercups through which they have tramped.

NOTE
- the emphasis on warmth and life in the reference to the flowers, and in their colours
- the sense of foreboding captured in the personified attempt by the brambles to impede the men's progress
- the simile at line 18 which captures the animation of the men – their living being

Suddenly the mood changes. The men's souls and bodies tighten in preparation for battle. The signs are not those of alarm and haste but rather a lift of the eyes to the sun – 'like a friend' to whom adieus are taken. Have all of the men responded to this gift of life and of light?

Then at once the men 'topped the hill' and raced over the no-man's-land of the open stretch below. Fury opened up against them. The sky burned.

NOTE
- the strategic placement of 'Exposed' at the beginning of line 29. The word is as isolated and vulnerable in the line as the men are on the field.
- the connection established by alliteration between 'burned' and 'blood', between the gunfire that ripped into the peace of the sky and the decimated bodies of the men
- the suggestion in the enjambment of the line of the breathlessness of the men's race across the open space of ' herb and heather'
- the metaphorical evocation of the men's journey into the infinite space of death
- the emphasis on heat and the repeated reference to the 'fury' of the place – Nature as the aggressor against those who have turned their backs on the gifts it offered in stanzas 1 and 2
- the consciousness of God's presence
- the sense of wild chaos captured in the harsh assonance of 'ur' in 'burned' of line 29, 'upsurge' of line 35 and 'verge' of line 36

The final stanza poses a question to which the details of the poem provide the answer even if the survivors of this holocaust are themselves silent. How effective is the extended hell metaphor? What explanation does it give of the survivors' silence?

Serenity is regained. Calm replaces the fury just past. Has night fallen?

The techniques

Consider the contribution made to the development of the poem's ideas and subject matter by:
- tactile, visual and auditory images
- the use of rhyme
- the use of assonance
- the use of contrast

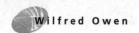

- the sense of time and of timelessness
- the symbolic use of fire to define the horror of the battlefield experience
- the symbolism of flowers – the buttercups are symbols of peace but are also the receptacles of blood
- the symbolic reference to cups – buttercups, chalices, communion cups
- the symbolic association of light with God
- structure
- effective word placement

The themes

Consider the following thematic possibilities
- the hell that is war
- the inability or unwillingness of soldiers who have survived the horrors of war to enunciate their experience
- the waste of life that is the inevitable consequence of war
- a soldier's capacity to sense his own death
- the exhilaration and heightened expectation of war
- bloody sacrifice of men in war
- the importance of the soul

The universal elements

'Spring Offensive' presents war as an act of Nature whose gift of serenity is spurned by those who would engage in conflict.

YOUR SECOND RESPONSE

1. How successfully does Owen take the reader on an attack in 'Spring Offensive'?
2. '"Spring Offensive" deals with war in cosmic terms.' Analyse the achievement of Owen in this poem.
3. '"Spring Offensive" captures both the horror and exhilaration of war.' Do you agree?

'Music'

'Music' is evidence of what a poet can achieve within the confines of the sonnet form. It is a deeply-felt celebration of the emotional depths of the human spirit, captured in the imagery of music. Like a classical musician, Owen worked on many drafts of the poem before he was satisfied with the final performance.

BEFORE YOU READ

- Revise the principles of sonnet form.
- Listen to a selection of classical and military music so that you are able to iden-tify, in your inner ear, the sounds of the violin, the organ, pipes and flutes, drums, gongs and oboes. Include at least one symphony in your selection.
- Revise the principles of metre, rhyme and imagery.

YOUR FIRST RESPONSE

A CLOSER ANALYSIS

The opening statement of the poem introduces an immediate sense of melan-choly and nostalgia, an acknowledgment of the sadnesses that have been the speaker's experience. At the same time, the words acknowledge that the flesh and the spirit that is this man is receptive of the 'urg[ing]' of violins, that his being has the capacity for deep feeling. The round, plaintive 'ow' sounds of the asso-nance of 'mellow sorrows' and the repetition of 'sorrows' enunciate the fullness of the pain this awareness has brought him. The minor key and sound combina-tion of 'slake' is disturbing: an intimation of agony. The depth of feelings the word evokes is emphasised further by the pre-eminence given to it by its place-ment at the end of the line.

The speaker's feelings of pain and anguish are strong and persistent. They demand the strength of expression of monosyllables. Such firm spoken acknowl-edgment of them, however, has its own awfulness. The pain of experience remains close to the surface.

The grammatical conjunction of 'sorrows' and 'sins' in line 3 underlines the speaker's recognition of the causal link between the two. Is it not an acknowl-edgment also of humankind's history of suffering attributable to original sin? A universalising of the speaker's experience?

What is the achievement of the enjambment of the first three lines of this first quatrain? The creation of a sense of languid resignation? The evocation of regret? A suggestion of the long expanses of time in which the speaker has been beset with sorrows and the consciousness of his sin?

The last line of the first quatrain records the active agony that is the conse-quence of those matters outlined in the first three lines. The image is not only musical – it is also military.

The emotion of the poem swells with the first phrase of line five. The image captures the welling heart, the exhortation which '[h]uge chords' have induced in the speaker's soul – as indeed they do ours. The colon introduces the human response to such prompting of the spirit: violent actions expressing the darkness which lurk inside us all. How is the intensity of this violence conveyed in the repetition of the heavy 'ud' sounds of line 6? How well does the assonance combine with the classical imagery of 'god's thunder'? Have the big drums now intruded into the lighter, if shriller sounds of the violins?

The drama of the great sound of awful actions wrought in great anger is muted almost as quickly as the swiftness of its outburst on the stage of the speaker's experience. The conjunction of line 6 and the softer sounds of 'pondered' record the spent nature of the previous feelings of great energy and control. The mood changes swiftly with the enjambment of lines 6 and 7 to one of philosophical contemplation of a world that is chaotic and cursed. It is a dark universe in which the speaker lives and breathes and feels. Even the winds are beggared ('maundered') as they, too, wander the earth. The last line of the octave is muted, sad; the atmosphere is of one of aimless loss.

The sestet introduces a contrasting movement with its emphasis on gaiety and laughter. The 'fifes' are high-pitched – yet also 'trivial'. What is the effect of this description of them? An implied statement of their unimportance? Of the brevity and insignificance of the speaker's (and any individual's) moments of joy? The almost full pause marked by the semicolon at the end of the line suggests that this is so – or at least these moments of joy are isolated from general common experience.

Yet there are also 'sweet' songs in life – and ridiculous absurdities represented by the 'gongs' and the 'oboes'. There *is* laughter. Yet there are other matters in being, existing beyond the introspection and separate experience of the individual. These are introduced by the dramatic qualification of the 'Yet' of line 11. They are the delightful riches gained from love and from loving, from the warmth of the individual's relationship with another.

The range of musical images in the poem is brought together with the image of 'Life's symphony' in line 12. Again, this image is given pre-eminence by its placement in the poetic line. The excitement of the lovers' responses to the speaker's touch, conveyed in the images of the beating hearts and the 'trembling cries' of 'Love's body' energises the poem. Their generalities are brought to a gentler personal focus in the singularity of the private moment of the last line. The subtleties conjured up in the image are developed by the alliterative use of 'l' and 's' sounds.

How effectively have these images and ideas of the sestet balanced the sorrowing melancholy of the octave? Are there not significant resonances between the two? Echoes of the 'brave drum' and the 'thuds of gods' thunder' in the 'beat' of the hearts and the gentle violence of the touches of love? What is the achievement of the parallel that is established between the wandering of the 'low lost winds' (and the softness of the utterance) and the blowing on 'my love's lips'? Merely a quiet denouement to the activity of the previous lines in both cases, or more than this?

What is the significance of the last word of the sonnet being given to 'sighs'? Is the conclusion of the poem bitter sweet?

The techniques

Consider the contribution of the following techniques to the development of the subject matter and theme:

- the use of sonnet form, including the effect of the rhyme (including the rhyming couplet with which the poem concludes) and of the space division between the octave and the sestet
- the use of enjambment
- the use of alliteration and assonance
- the range of the imagery and its 'collection' in the image of the symphony
- the contrast established between the rhythm of the octave and the sestet by the relative predominance of monosyllables in the octave
- the resonances created by the repetition of words and ideas and images especially between the stanzas
- the classical sense given to the imagery by the reference to 'gods' thunder' and to love

The themes

Consider the following thematic possibilities:

- the emotional complexity of humankind
- the struggle and suffering that is inherent in existence – its relationship with the sinful nature of huma kind; original sin
- the cruelty of the world
- the human penchant for violence
- the power of music to soothe the savage breast – and of love to soothe the savage beast
- the thirst of man (as opposed to woman) kind for power, dominance and control – both of the world and of their partners
- the sense of the world as an empty universe in which the gods (formerly Gods) have been reduced to angry and wilful expressions of power for meaningless purpose
- humankind's craving for intimacy
- the joys – and pains of love

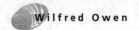

The universal elements

The poem reworks classical and traditional imagery in a classical poetic form in order to make a statement about the very nature of humankind. It explores both the darkness and the lightness of the heart and the soul.

While not specifically dealing with war, this poem does present the passions in which all wars have their origins – the thirst for anger, regret, and the subjugation of love to the lust for power.

YOUR SECOND RESPONSE

1. 'Music' introduces the reader to the passions of humankind which resurface in Owen's maturer poetry. Do you agree?
2. Is this a 'war' poem? Is it more about violence – the foundation of all wars – than it is about love?
3. Is 'Music' too finely crafted a poem to be fully effective in its exploration of the universal themes of love and war?
4. What evidence is there in 'Music' that Owen is a significant poet?

4

Preparing successfully for exams

Using quotations effectively

A successful discussion of poetry requires an effective illustration of its use of language and imagery in creating its atmosphere and in developing its themes. This can often be achieved only by the integration of quotations into your discussion. Effective use of quotation will demonstrate an awareness of the following points:

- Short, direct quotations, included in quotation marks and fluently integrated into your own discussion, are usually the most effective.
- A full stop is placed at the end of a short quote if the sentence ending coincides with the end of the quote. Otherwise, the punctuation of the sentence which contains the quote is uninterrupted.
- Short quotations should not be indented as this practice will interrupt the flow of your ideas.
- Quotations of more than two or three lines should be indented so that they are visually distinct from the text of your discussion. Indented quotations do not have to be included in quotation marks. To continue your discussion after their use, you should start the next line of your writing against the left margin.
- Long quotations can be abbreviated by omitting words and replacing them with and ellipsis (…), the standard indication of an omission. Make sure that the words you do include contribute to and follow the context of your discussion.
- Any adjustments to a quotation to fit the context of your own discussion should be included in square brackets: [ ].
- Any explanation of the quotation's meaning or relevance to the argument, if included within the quotation, should be enclosed in parentheses: ( ).

Remember that quotations should enhance your discussion and illustrate or assist the development of your argument. They will not save a weak argument or replace your own effective discussion of ideas.

Some tips for exam preparation

As you prepare for poetry examinations, remember these points:

- Follow the syllabus and gain a working knowledge of each poem set for study on your course. Do **not** try to second guess the examiners as to the individual poems they will ask you to write on, or the features of them they will emphasise.
- Give some structure to your revision of each poem by organising its themes into a hierarchy of significance or interest. Do not feel obliged to discuss each poem in the same depth, but do note the development of the theme throughout the poem.
- A fully effective discussion of themes requires you to examine the techniques of language (including assonance, alliteration, rhyme and metrical patterns) and imagery used to develop them.
- Identify the pattern of imagery developed in the poem and note its expansion of the poem's ideas.
- Identify any symbols used by the poet and the range of their possible meanings.
- Consider how the atmosphere and setting of the poem contribute to its meaning and to the conveying of the poet's message.
- Consider the sounds of the poem – poetry is, after all, sound with meaning.

As well as studying the poems, make time during your preparation to polish up the basics of essay structure. You exam answer should by restricted to a range of properly illustrated points in an essay which has an effective introduction; interlinking paragraphs each developing one major idea; and an effective conclusion. This is a good start to earning high marks.

Don't overburden yourself with quotations, and remember: answer the question!

An essay plan for writing an effective examination answer on a poem

Part 1	Part 2	Part 3
Contents	Themes	Your reactions (a) Your response to technical aspects (b) Your response to emotional aspects

Part 1:Contents

In your first paragraph(s), briefly retell the contents of the poem. That is, in your own words, outline the scene, action or general situation presented by the poet. During this initial section, also briefly discuss any interesting genres used by the poet, and any interesting literary devices such as similes, metaphors, pararhyme, personifications etc which allowed the poem's contents to be easily imagined by you.

Part 2:Themes

In the second paragraph(s) of your essay, outline the various themes or central ideas that the poet is presenting or exploring in his poem. Remember you may identify more than one theme in a poem which you consider merits discussion. Where possible, you should identify the hierarchy or relative importance of the themes.

Part 3:Your reactions

In the final paragraphs (which should be the main section of your essay) discuss your reactions to the poem. You may approach this section on two levels.

(a) Your reactions to the technical aspects of the poem. Here you may consider such questions as:

(i) Has the poem any vivid or graphic images? By what means does the poet define his subject matter?

(ii) Does the poet use any interesting sound devices which help to reinforce or indeed become part of the poem's central ideas?

(iii) What is interesting or memorable about the poet's choice of words (poetic diction) and their arrangement into poetic lines (syntax)? What significance can be attached to the placement in the poetic line of particular words and phrases? Of the repetition of particular words and phrases?

(iv) Does the poem's overall rhythm add to its effectiveness? Does the poem 'low' or is its rhythm disjointed at times for particular effect? What contribution is made to the poem's effect by the poet's choice of rhyme?

(v) Does the poet use any interesting devices such as direct speech, slang, foreign words or phrases, particularly horrifying and graphic words and phrases, direct personal questioning or other rhetorical techniques? What is their contribution to theme?

(vi) Does the poet stimulate more than our visual senses? Does he include descriptions or tactile, taste, smell and auditory reactions?

(b) In discussing your reactions to the emotional aspects of the poem, range over your response to the poem's themes, and atmosphere. You may wish to consider some of the following questions in formulating your ideas:

(i) How dramatic are the ideas expressed by the poet? How moving? How intensely personal? Do they have universal application beyond the immediate setting of the poem?

(ii) Is the poet's tone of voice powerful and persuasive? Is he didactic? Does he demand the attention of our imagination?

(iii) Is the overall atmosphere or mood of the poem consistent throughout the poem or does it change? How much is it also a part of the poem's meaning?

(iv) Does any aspect of the poem have a particular personal relevance to your own experience or study, or, alternatively, have a particularly profound effect on you?

Some general points to consider and general pitfalls to avoid

1. The exam question may ask you to include in your analysis of one or more poems of your chosen poet, a consideration of how the poem(s) which you choose to discuss is/are generally characteristic of the poet's works. Ideally, you should discuss such characteristics in their appropriate section; ie technical characteristics in paragraph 1 and thematic characteristics in paragraph 2. It is, however, acceptable to include a short separate paragraph on such characteristics between paragraphs 3 and 4. Whatever approach you choose, don't merely supply a shopping list. Illustrate each characteristic with quotes, examples and brief references to other poems.

2. Stick to the task of analysing your chosen poem(s) in terms of the question. Don't waste time discussing in general terms the analysis of poetry or, worse still, how much you dislike doing it.

3. Don't devote a whole separate paragraph for the mere listing of literary devices used in a poem. When you do write about any particular device, don't just state that it is there. For example, 'In the fourth and fifth lines, Owen uses assonance.' Go on to say how effective the use of this device is and what the poet contributes to his development of theme and atmosphere in employing it. Does it add drama? Intensify the thought? Shock? Surprise? Awaken the imagination?

4. When you chose to criticise a poem, do so in a constructive and subtle manner. Avoid outlandish rude statements and unsupported generalisations. On the other hand, avoid forced or obvious exaggerated enthusiasm. Avoid

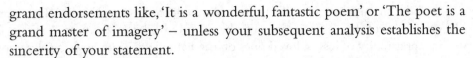

grand endorsements like, 'It is a wonderful, fantastic poem' or 'The poet is a grand master of imagery' – unless your subsequent analysis establishes the sincerity of your statement.

5. Remember to use the conventions of quoting lines from the poems and integrating them into your discussion.

6. Avoid spelling, grammar and punctuation errors. A simple thought, properly expressed and correctly spelt and simply endorsed by an effective selection of a short quotation is much more effective than long, convoluted sentences which evidence an affected and insincere writing style adopted especially for the examination.

Exam topics and guides to answers

Topic 1

'The Great War produced some great poetry.' Discuss the achievement of Wilfred Owen in the light of this comment.

This question invites you to make your own selection from the poems which you have studied in order to illustrate and support your critical assessment of Owen's work. Be careful that you do not attempt to analyse too many poems so that your answer is too superficial. Be careful, too, that your discussion of Owen's achievement is not restricted to an analysis merely of his themes. Consider also the importance of atmosphere and tone and the range of characters covered in his work. Consider the techniques exploited by Owen in developing each of these.

CHECKLIST

In your answer, you might like to:
- consider Owen's capacity to capture both individual suffering as well as the individual horror of the battlefield in poems like 'The Sentry' and 'The Show' and 'Dulce et Decorum Est.' Consider the sentry's blind panic; the dramatic desperation of both him and his officer who narrates the events which he is powerless to prevent. Note the continuing resonance of the sentry's personal tragedy – and especially his voiced hopelessness in the officer's imagination. Consider the gargoyle effect of the gassed man in 'Dulce et Decorum Est', his isolation from those who were able to find their gas masks in time; the prolonged nature of his suffering and the noise of it, even after his death. Note the echo of the bloodied feet of his companions in the bloody froth that gargled from his lungs with every jolt of the wagon into which his corpse was flung. Feel the shock of the persona's realisation of his own mutilation and death in 'The Show'.

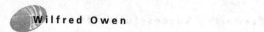

- consider the achievement of Owen in 'Anthem for Doomed Youth'. The appropriateness of his exploitation of the elevated sonnet form to express the inexpressibility of loss of loved ones on the battlefield. Note how the alliteration and assonance of the poem bring home the noise of the battlefield to mock civil celebration of a soldier's death.
- analyse Owen's capacity to capture the pessimism and sense of hopelessness of the battlefield and to humanise the appalling war casualty statistics in 'the Sentry', Strange Meeting', 'Anthem for Doomed Youth', 'Dulce et Decorum Est'
- analyse Owen's special use of Romantic elements, including the May landscape, in 'Spring Offensive'

Topic 2

'Owen achieved beautiful poetry whilst writing about the horrors of war.' Discuss.

This question invites you to discuss the development of Owen's imagery of the battlefield and the poetic quality of his description of the horrors of war.

CHECKLIST

In your answer, you might like to:
- analyse Owen's poetic achievement in 'The Show' or 'Mental Cases'. Both poems do not sacrifice poetic finesse to the gruesome pictures which they elaborate.
- consider the extended image in 'Miners'
- consider the unusual effect and meaning of sunlight in 'Futility' and 'Spring Offensive'.
- analyse Owen's special concentration on faces as individual expressions of the horrors of war in 'Spring offensive', 'The Show', 'Dulce et Decorum Est', 'Strange meeting' and 'Mental Cases'
- consider the particular effect of assonance and alliteration in 'Anthem for Doomed Youth'
- consider Owen's use of pararhyme in a range of his poems
- analyse the dramatic and blunt evocation of personal experience in 'The Sentry'

Topic 3

'Owen demonstrates the cult of patriotism to be a false creed.' Discuss.

Owen placed no direct blame for the carnage that was World War I on the generals or the politicians or the civilians who espoused it as a Great Adventure, yet in portraying it as a human catastrophe beyond the comprehension of these, he denounced the simplicity and hopeless romanticism of their view. Some of his poems reflect more clearly than others this gulf of understanding which would always exist between those who knew (and even survived) the horrors of the battlefield and those who sent a whole generation of British youth to suffer and die there.

CHECKLIST

In your discussion of this topic, you might like to consider:

* the achievement of Owen in 'Anthem for Doomed Youth', and in particular, this poem's definition of the contrasting wariness between civilian and soldier of death on the battlefield, and the inadequate recognition of soldiers' suffering in civilian rituals of mourning
* the condemnation of all warfare as an offensive against nature as well against the enemy in 'Spring Offensive'
* the dramatic intensity of the climactic statement of 'Dulce et Decorum Est' and that poem's imaginative support of it
* the shocking universal statement of the wasteful carnage of war presented in 'The Show' and more simply but just as effectively in 'Futility'
* the pathos and sense of wasted youth evoked in 'Disabled'
* the unassuageable grief expressed in 'Insensibility'

Topic 4

'Owen saw himself as a news bearer, yet brought a particular intensity of vision and tragic quality to the scenes of war he sent home in his poetry.' Analyse Owen's achievement in these terms.

This question invites you to evaluate the achievement of Owen as a recorder of the facts of the battlefield. It invites you to consider the accuracy and detail of the battlefield scenes captured in his work. In doing so, you may well be struck by the particular dramatic intensity of these pictures and by the tragic vision they presented of Owen's particular, and indeed of all war. The best discussion of this topic will include a consideration of the range of imagery of selected poems, of their allegorical or universal elements, of the fine evocation of emotion by the poet's capturing of the grotesque reality of the battlefield.

CHECKLIST

In answering this question, you may like to consider:

* the personal suffering evoked through graphic description in 'the Sentry' and 'Dulce et Decorum Est'
* the shock tactics of 'Spring Offensive'
* the mud and slaughter captured in 'the Sentry', 'The Show', 'Dulce et Decorum Est'

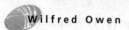

- the noisy reality of death presented in 'Anthem for Doomed Youth' and 'Spring Offensive'
- the powerful personal tragedy of the disabled in 'Mental Cases' and 'Disabled'

More focus questions

Here are some more focus questions for you to use as a starting point for your own analysis of Owen's work. (You will find some clues to assist you in developing your own response to them in the previous material. Remember, though, that a well-informed and thoughtful original response is always the best.)

1. 'Poetry is the exploitation of intense experience.' Discuss with reference to Owen's work.

2. 'It is the individual soldiers of Owen's poems who remain in our memory long after we have met them, not the grotesque landscapes of World War I.' Do you agree?

3. 'Owen makes remarkable poetry out of the greatest human tragedy of the twentieth century.' Discuss three or four of Owen's poems in the light of this statement, concentrating equally on theme and technique.

4. Examine the journalistic element in Owen's poetry. Does it contribute to or mar the poet's final achievement?

5. Demonstrate the variety of Owen's poetic voice and the variety of emotions explored by it.

6. Heroism, honour, idealism, patriotism – are any of these to be found in Owen's poems. Are they lauded or derided?

7. Can a poet of World War I have any lasting thing to say to us? Discuss at least two poems in your answer.

8. Owen's poetic sympathies lie with the survivors rather than the victims of war whose deaths came quickly if grotesquely. Do you agree?

9. Owen brings us face to face with war. He forces us to look upon the maimed and the dying, to confront the ugliness of corpses and to run the gamut of deadly artillery fire, to face the sense of hopelessness felt by man when faced with one of the world's greatest evils – war. Using these statements as an introductory paragraph, evaluate Owen's achievement as a poet.